D1596240

the mystery
of christian hope

the mystery of christian hope

Translated by M. Angeline Bouchard

Jean galot s.J.

ALBA · HOUSE   alba house   NEW · YORK

SOCIETY OF ST. PAUL, 2187 VICTORY BLVD., STATEN ISLAND, NEW YORK 10314

Library of Congress Cataloging in Publication Data

Galot, Jean.
    The mystery of Christian hope.

    Translation of Le mystere de l'espérance.
    Includes bibliographical references.
    1. Hope. I. Title.
BV4638.G3413   234'.2   77-1222
ISBN 0-8189-0346-5

Nihil Obstat:

Daniel V. Flynn, J.C.D.
Censor Librorum

Imprimatur:

✠ **James P. Mahoney, D.D.**
Vicar General, Archdiocese of New York
January 22, 1977

Designed, printed and bound in the United States of
America by the Fathers and Brothers of the Society of St. Paul,
2187 Victory Boulevard, Staten Island, New York, 10314,
as part of their communications apostolate.

1 2 3 4 5 6 7 8 9 (Current Printing: first digit).

TABLE OF CONTENTS

the mystery of christian hope

CHAPTER I

HOPE IN CRISIS

The Present Crisis of Hope

Faith and hope are under greater challenge whenever thinking and social structures are in a state of profound change. Our own era clearly faces a crisis of faith. In particular, the trend to secularization is triggering a transition from institutional faith to a more individual, personal faith. Such an evolution cannot fail to occasion certain deviations, uncertainties, and defections. Not a few Christians have begun to ask themselves what kind of a God they believe in, what kind of a God they should believe in. Some are even being lured into an unbelief whose "positive" aspects are made to appear attractive.

No less deep and fundamental is the crisis of hope. The mutation seems so basic that it forces us to ask new questions about the future. What will the Church of tomorrow be like? And tomorrow's Christians? What is the ultimate destiny of mankind? And what is the mysterious world beyond death really like, stripped of its mythological imagery?

Man's conception of the future has a determining influence on his behavior. For he makes his choices not only in the light of what he believes concerning present reality, but in the context of what he expects of the future. If he maintains his hope by holding to a positive vision of the future he can overcome his current doubts.

If he stops hoping, he is swept away by his own weakness, imprisoned in his despair, and cannot see beyond the limited horizons of his life here and now. As a result, his mind grows weary, and his thoughts become narrow, perhaps even rebellious. A bitterly critical person runs the risk of walling himself up in his own views, with no chance of reaching out to a solution or to salvation.

Many Catholics who have been startled out of a traditionalism that accepted the Church **in toto** without thinking its problems out individually, are inclined to condemn the Church and formulate strongly critical views about it. We should not be surprised or scandalized at criticisms of a society that is made up of sinners, especially if these criticisms are self-criticism born of the realization that all the members of the Church are one body and each member has a responsibility to the whole. Just as we all receive a share in God's holiness as his people, so, too, we are invited to acknowledge our sins, correct our mistakes, and ask God's forgiveness for the scandals we have caused.

The situation grows more serious when the critic challenges the hope that the Church bears within it. Has this Church proved incapable of being what it should be? Has it failed in its mission? Can it still expect to attain the goal that is the reason for its existence? Has it not fallen short of transforming the world or even of making authentic Christians of its own members? Has it not been caught in the very act of transgressing the principles of the Gospel? How can such a Church merit the hope of all mankind?

Without challenging the Church's indefectibility, there are some who would restrain its ambitions. They see the Church of the future consisting of a relative handful of believers, faithful witnesses dispersed in a world alien to Christianity, humbly bearing witness to the presence of Christ's love. Seen in this perspective the Church no longer stands out as the vital force progressively introducing the Gospel message to all men, permeating both social structures and individuals until the whole world has become Christian.

As a result of such thinking, there are those for whom the obstacles seem too great and who turn to some other outlet for their hope. Some are tempted to hope in a Church that no longer focuses solely on dispensing spiritual salvation and showing the way to eternal life, but concerned above all with earthly and material tasks, with the well-being and happiness of people here and now. Under this aspect, the Gospel message, with its implications of social revolution, appears to be the bearer of a new hope, one that is more easily accessible to our contemporaries and more appealing in its short-term promises.

In and through the Church, it is Christ himself who is challenged by the crisis of hope. Are we still to think of Christ as the One who sums up within himself the entire hope of the world? And more specifically, as the Son of God who has become a member of the human community in order to transform it through his divine and yet fully incarnate action? Some are inclined to found all their hopes on man. Everything that is "supernatural" seems to them adventitious, artificial, incompatible with a secularized world. They wonder whether hope might not profit by discarding its Christian character and being reduced to a purely human hope, a hope founded on man's capacities.

Living In Despair

Underlying the present-day crisis of hope we find a current of existentialistic philosophy which has disseminated the notion that the world and all human existence are absurd. This trend has inserted despair into the very notion of being, making it a fundamental and inseparable element of existence. We shall limit ourselves to a few succinct remarks on the subject, as it would be superfluous to offer still another analysis of these philosophical doctrines.

At the origin of the existentialist movement, Kierkegaard's 19th century existentialism sheds light on the origin of existential despair in terms of a religious mentality dominated by deep-seated anxiety vis-à-vis God.

Such was the religion of Kierkegaard's father, imprisoned in a strict Lutheranism and undermined by secret and irremediable anxieties. To quote the philosopher: "The worst danger is not that the father . . . is a free thinker, or even a hypocrite. No, it is that he is a devout man, full of the fear of God, and the child is convinced, certain, yet senses a hidden anxiety within his father, as if neither fear of God nor piety could give him peace."[1]

At first the child was filled with admiration for his father, in whom he saw the ideal incarnation of a Christian life. One day he discovered his father was a sinner constantly trembling under God's wrath who, despite all his efforts to cling to God, was incapable of inner happiness. "It was then the great earthquake took place, the terrible upheaval which suddenly imposed a new law upon me for infallibly interpreting all phenomena. It was then I detected my father's advanced years were not a blessing from God but rather a curse; that the eminent intellectual gifts of our family were only for their mutual extirpation. It was then I felt the silence of death grow all around me, when my father appeared to me as an ill-starred man who was outliving all of us like a cross on the grave of his own hopes. If a sin weighed upon the whole family, if a punishment of God hovered over it, then the family would disappear, destroyed by his omnipotence, wiped out like an abortive effort, and it was only very rarely that I found solace in the thought that my father had had the burdensome duty of pacifying us through the consolations of religion."[2]

The new law for the infallible interpretation of all phenomena acknowledges despair as a kind of dialectical necessity. "We speak of despair as if there were only a few individuals in this state," whereas this is really a universal state. "The world is despair, and does not know it."[3] In his work **Sickness unto Death** Kierkegaard has analyzed the forms of despair. "Despair is sin."[4] It consists either in not wanting to be oneself, or in wanting to be oneself, while detaching oneself from God. When we read this treatise on despair, we get the impression the author is describing an attitude he condemns but that he himself is experiencing, and whose psychological depths he can therefore better describe.

The primordial root of this existential despair is his doubt concerning God's love, inherited from his father's religion. In his view, despair tends to shut a man up within himself, but it can be understood only within the context of man's relations with God.

Man's relationship to God, which Kierkegaard vigorously stressed, is discarded in the existentialism of Heidegger, Sartre, and Camus. For them despair somehow succeeds in focussing man's attention on himself because God no longer exists. There is only human existence left, no longer facing a Creator but confronting itself.

According to Heidegger, to exist is to find oneself in a state of dereliction, of abandonment. To his mind, anguish introduces us into authentic existence because it reveals nothingness. The interpretation of this nothing-

ness as the nullity of the sinner before God and the idea
of a Redemption destined to wipe out this misery simply
camouflages the true meaning of anguish.[5]

Sartre depicts the nausea that results from absolute
absurdity: "We were a bunch of existents, hampered and
encumbered by ourselves. Not one of us had the slightest
reason for being there, each confused, vaguely disturbed
existent felt he was superfluous in relation to others . . .
And—feeble, languishing, obscene, digesting, tossing
about mournful thoughts—I, too, was superfluous . . . I
had vague dreams of doing away with myself, in order
to annihilate at least one of these superfluous existences.
But even my death would have been superfluous. My
cadaver would have been superfluous . . . And the
gnawed flesh would have been too much for the earth
to hold, and my bones at last, cleaned, stripped, bright
and shining like teeth, would also have been too much:
I was superfluous for eternity."[6]

Quite as characteristic as the title of Sartre's novel,
Nausea, is the title of Camus' **The Plague.**[7] Camus shows
us our world under the features of the city of Oran, laid
low by the ravages of pestilence and cut off from all contact with the outside, a world condemned to undergo
fearful sufferings that do not even spare innocent children and belie the Christian explanation of calamities
in the light of God's justice. No hope is given this world
from above. All anyone can do is protest against an
absurd destiny, and try, like the doctor in the novel, to
bring some relief to those who are undergoing it.

The Crisis in the Hope of the Jews

It will help us to understand our own crisis if we call
to mind the crises of hope the Jewish people experienced.
What Scripture tells us of these crises has a certain

meaning for us, even though the coming of Christ turned the conditions of human hope topsy-turvy.

Exodus was an adventure that challenged not only the faith but also the hope of the Jewish people. At the origin of the adventure was God's plan to liberate his people and lead them "into a good and spacious land, a land flowing with milk and honey" (Ex 3:8). This plan gave a basis for hope by offering the supreme guarantee of the covenant. God said to Moses: "I will be with you" (Ex 3:12). It was precisely this promise that the Jews began to doubt when they found themselves faced with the privations of the desert. "Is the Lord in our midst or not?" (Ex 17:7). The manna and the water gushing from the rock were given as visible signs of God's help. The crises of hope that broke out in the form of grumbling assumed what might be called a classic form. What the people were challenging was the truth of the covenant, God's fidelity to his promise. It can be affirmed that every crisis of hope, in the last analysis, can be summed up in the question: "Is God with us?"

In our present-day crisis of hope, the challenge addresses itself to the truth and fidelity of the divine covenant as incarnated in the Church. The fundamental question is this: "Is God with us through the Church, or is the Church powerless to express and guarantee the efficacious presence of God?"

For the Jewish people, the Exile was the most keenly felt national disaster, the most terrible of trials for their hope. They looked upon the deportation to Babylon as a punishment inflicted on them because of their sins. As a result, instead of being driven to despair they were inspired to expect a more generous liberation. The prophets certainly stressed the might of God's punishment, but they likewise pointed to the merciful intention that motivated it. They made the Jews realize their infidelity could cause no doubt as to God's fidelity to the Covenant:

"For I know well the plans I have in mind for you, says the Lord, plans for your welfare, not for woe! plans to give you a future full of hope" (Jr 29:11). Hope was thus promised at the very moment tribulation was at its worst. The restoration would reveal the triumph of hope.

Like Exodus, the Exile draws our attention to a perennial cause of the crisis of hope: mankind's sins. However, in the divine plan the consequences of sin need not be totally negative. The sins of men can be the occasion for a rebirth of trust, more firmly rooted than before on the gratuity of God's mercy. Every acknowledgment of infidelity to God should be accompanied by awareness of "a future full of hope."

The severity of personal trials need not drive men to despair either. Even the most heavily burdened and anguishing person is called to "renew" his hope, in the words of the author of the **Lamentations:** "The favors of the Lord are not exhausted, his mercies are not spent; they are renewed each morning, so great is his faithfulness. My portion is the Lord, says my soul; therefore will I hope in him" (Lm 3:22-24). In the midst of every kind of misfortune, the conviction remains that in the end God's goodness will win out over wrath: "For the Lord's rejection does not last forever; though he punishes, he takes pity, in the abundance of his mercies; he has no joy in afflicting or grieving the sons of men" (Lm 3:31-33).

The decisive value of hope lies in the fact that it is identified with God. The Lord is invoked as "O Hope of Israel, O Lord, our savior in time of need!" (Jr 14:8). Jeremiah's words contain the solution to all crises of hope: "You are my hope!" (cf. Jr 17:14).

Clearly, therefore, the hope that succeeds in overcoming all difficulties is not a humanly-founded hope of some sort. It is hope founded on God. This distinction keeps us from confusing false hopes with authentic hope.

The beatitude of the man who hopes in God deserves thoughtful meditation: "Blessed is the man who trusts in the Lord, whose hope is the Lord. He is like a tree planted beside the waters that stretches out its roots to the stream: it fears not the heat when it comes, its leaves stay green; in the year of drought it shows no distress, but still bears fruit" (Jr 17:7-8). Crises are overcome in advance through a firm hope in the Lord God.

And yet the hope of the Jews ran headlong against a formidable obstacle: death. Their hope was limited to earthly life and within this unduly restricted area the suffering of the just man posed a problem not easily solved. The Book of Job emphasized this problem. Job's hope held firm in the midst of trials and tribulations, but since it could not venture beyond death it could not dispel the obscurity surrounding God's final intervention. In Job, as in the case of certain Psalmists,[8] we find "the certitude that communion with the living God prevails in advance over all the powers of death."[9] However, Job's question: "when man expires, where then is he?" (Jb 14:10) remains unanswered.[10] It was only a short time before the coming of Jesus that hope emerged finally as the affirmation of a blessed immortality.

The First Crisis of Christian Hope

The first crisis of Christian hope occurred at a most important moment in the foundation of Christianity, between the death and the Resurrection of Christ.

When Jesus repeatedly announced that the death of the Son of man would be followed by his Resurrection, he was striving to inspire his disciples with an attitude of hope. The event of the Transfiguration, which anticipated the Resurrection in a striking way, was directed to the same end. When we read the declarations recorded in the Fourth Gospel in the discourse after the Last Supper, we see that on the eve of his death Christ's dominant concern was to kindle hope among his friends. He assured them that his absence would last only a little while, and they would soon see him again. Even while foretelling the sadness they were about to experience, he assured them that it would be changed into joy. When he said to them: "Have faith in God and faith in me" (Jn 14:1), he was calling for a faith that looked to the future and was completely imbued with hope. In the terms John uses, it appears Jesus was also addressing himself to all future generations: "But take courage! I have overcome the world" (Jn 16:33).

Now, the Master's admonitions did not have the hoped-for effect on the first disciples at the time of his death. It is evident their hope had foundered when we see how hard it was for them to accept the reality of the Resurrection, and when we note how the risen Christ reproached them for their unbelief. The disciples who walked with Jesus on the road to Emmaus spoke of a lost hope: "We were hoping that he was the one who would set Israel free. Besides all this, today, [is] the third day since these things happened" (Lk 24:21).

The disciples' words are very indicative: the great trial of the Passion had destroyed their hope. Jesus had not been able to inspire his followers with a hope that would stand firm for even three days and lead them to accept the Resurrection. We can see in this a sign of the future crises of hope that would haunt the whole life of the Church and especially those epochs when it would be living the Passion of Christ most intensely amid persecution, scorn or failure.

Within the group of the Twelve, two incidents illustrate this crisis of hope. The tragedy of Judas doubtless began in the stirring of another kind of hope, the hope of an abundance of material goods that would supplant the hope of the spiritual kingdom. It ended in a despair that is recorded in one of the most poignant pages of the Gospel. Obviously, it was not his odious betrayal of the Master that was Judas' undoing. What destroyed him was the final act by which he refused to turn for help to the one whose merciful kindness he had so often personally witnessed.

Peter's tragedy stemmed from the fact that he founded his hope in his own will and human resources. The Apostle learned through a humiliating and heartrending experience how vain was this presumption. There is a perennial value in the lesson given the man who was destined to be the first head of the Church. Any hope that relies solely on human resources and on the strength of the human will is in danger of collapse.

When we try to explain Peter's attitudes, we must say that his hope also differed from genuine Christian hope because it aspired to an earthly kingdom, to be conquered by the sword. When Jesus held back his arm, he brought down this hope. At the very moment when Jesus could have benefited from the use of Peter's weapon for his own defense, he gave decisive witness that his kingdom is not of this world, and that it cannot turn to the means used by a political state in order to grow and flourish. The Church can depend for its future only on the spiritual power granted to it by God. That is why the hope of the Church cannot be triumphalist. Triumphalism would express trust in other than supernatural resources, and tend to assimilate the Church to political societies.

There is much food for meditation in the fact that Jesus clearly diverted Peter from a political conception of the kingdom. Hope is easily tempted to aspire to a future for the Church assured by a position of strength within human society. Christ has definitively rejected this course.

In contrast to this deviation of hope, the Evangelist Luke gives us an example of authentic hope, the new hope that was born at the instant of Jesus' death. The thief who asked Jesus to receive him in his kingdom could be thinking only of a kingdom not of this world, a kingdom beyond death. It was as though his spiritual poverty, his awareness of having made a failure of his life by turning to thievery, enabled him to surrender himself to a hope more firmly rooted in Christ.

The value of this attitude is apparent in the contrast with his fellow-robber's who refused to acknowledge his sin and his spiritual bankruptcy, and hence did not turn to Jesus for help. The Gospel narrative indicates to us that from that time onward, men would take sides in the presence of the salvation Christ offers, as between those who would hope and those who would refuse to hope.

The Challenges To Hope

Since the first crisis of Christian hope, there have been many others. The state of crisis is not an exceptional situation in the life of the Church. One might almost speak of a permanent crisis of hope that assumes different forms during each succeeding historical epoch. Inasmuch as hope is an essential element of Christian reality and this reality develops in a context of strife and opposition, hope may be said to be in a perpetual state of conflict.

Christian hope is constantly being challenged. Above all, there is the challenge of evil which persists and continues to stalk the world. Sin has never stopped spreading its contagion. We even sense that it tends to vaunt its exploits with ever greater insolence. If it sometimes hides in the shadows, at other times it shouts its identity in public, while trying to justify itself and be considered more acceptable. What impresses us is that sin always seems to attain greater extension and depth than anyone expected. Witness concentration camps, refinements of torture, multiplying acts of violence, and the vastly diverse ways the members of the human race exploit one another.

The spectacle of the rising tide of evil almost makes one doubt man is capable of moral progress. We cannot but wonder whether mankind has indeed been saved by Christ and whether the reign of love our Savior inaugurated is really spreading over the world.

The challenge to hope is even more keenly felt when evil seems to triumph among those who should be living witnesses to the holiness of Christ. It becomes harder to hope in the Church as the force destined to transform the world when we encounter dispositions contrary to the Gospel in those who represent the Church, whether members of the clergy or of the laity. We are disappointed to find the tactics of personal ambition in what should be the stronghold of service to the kingdom of Christ; malice, quarrels, acts of revenge among those in whom charity should be flourishing; greed and the feverish pursuit of money among those who should be giving the example of detachment from earthly possessions; hardness of heart, scorn for the weak and the poor among those very persons from whom we would most expect gentleness and respect for every human person. Even the strongest hope can be completely deflated by such discoveries.

The fact remains that the challenges to hope do not come entirely from outside us. There are some challenges to hope that come from within ourselves. Man is discouraged by the evil he sees in his own behavior. Not only does he not succeed in overcoming his faults, but he is often taken by surprise by feelings and actions beyond the control of his will. He feels he is being attacked within his own fortress and that he is powerless to resist. The more he learns about himself, the more he does discern in himself tendencies and motives that are far from praiseworthy. He has the sense of going backward instead of forward. Under such conditions can he honestly hold fast to the hope that divine life is flourishing within him? Every step backward, every disillusionment experienced with respect to his own behavior and attitudes tends to deny the validity of his hope, and to make him relegate it to the realm of utopias.

Failures of all sorts that make up the fabric of every human life also loom up as challenges to hope. No man succeeds as well as he might have anticipated or wished. Even if life brings him unexpected successes, it will also present him with unforeseen disappointments and failures somewhere along the way. Certain humiliations that we find hard to admit even to ourselves are very painful. They can lead to moral collapse, to a state of bitterness or rancor, and to deep discouragement. They are real challenges to our fidelity to Christian hope.

Psychologically, the phenomenon of mental depression expresses prostration under life's hardships and the inability to overcome them. There may be physical causes involved such as overwork and exhaustion. One's psychological attitudes may also play an important part. In any event, depression is a challenge from within an individual's temperament, directed against the victory of hope. The depressed person is inclined to despair. Obviously we should not confuse the optimism of a sanguine temperament with supernatural hope. For such hope is not necessarily absent even during a state of depression, but it is more difficult to maintain.

Going deeper still, a weariness with life, as it has been described by certain existential philosophers, can lead to despair. We are referring to a deep-seated boredom, an insatiability that penetrates to the deepest recesses of the human personality. It really amounts to ennui with regard to man's ultimate destiny, for he is made for God and can find his happiness only in God. Earthly life necessarily involves separation from God, and cannot offer man the final satisfaction of his desire for God. Saint Augustine has told of this experience, the restlessness of a heart that can find its rest only in God. In his case, unrest made his hope burn all the brighter. Even so, such anxiety constitutes a challenge to hope because it does not cease until death. The more deeply a man feels the need for God, the more he suffers from his inability to satisfy it. When he misjudges the reason for his malaise by denying the existence or the presence of God, he shuts himself up within his own being, only to be dismayed by his own incompleteness. Then his very existence seems absurd. Nothingness seems to be irremediably implanted at the very heart of his being.

This nothingness can also take on the aspect of suffering and death. Physical suffering appears to be a diminution of life, and as such is a challenge to the person. Psychological suffering makes the challenge to the person even deeper. Trials can descend upon a human life with such violence as to seem to crush the personality. Only hope can sustain the shock and keep the person from succumbing.

Finally, death is the ultimate challenge. It tends to eliminate all hope limited to earthly life, and allows only that hope to grow that leaps up into the world beyond. Death constitutes a test for all the aspirations that have governed a human life. The truth of death shows the small importance of certain things on which a person has centered his desires. It purifies hope by forcing it to become resolutely supernatural, directed toward values that last forever. For those who refuse to look upward death is a disaster, but for those who are ready to accept eternal life it is the final stimulus to a bold and total hope.

NOTES FOR CHAPTER ONE

1. **Journal**, 1850. Excerpt cited in the Introduction to his **Treatise on Despair**. (French translation, **Traité du désespoir**, by K. Ferlov, J. J. Gateau, 1949, p. 12).

2. **Journal**, French translation by Ferlov and Gateau, Paris, 1941, p. 110-111. Cf. P. Mesnard, **Le vrai visage de Kierkegaard**, 1948, p. 62-63.

3. **La maladie à la mort, Oeuvres complétes**, 16, Paris, 1971. French translation by P. H. Tisseau and E. M. Jacquet-Tisseau, p. 202. English translation by Walter Lowrie, Doubleday Anchor Books, 1955.

4. **Ibid.**, p. 235.

5. Cf. A. de Waelhens, **La philosopnie de Martin Heidegger**, Louvain, 1955, p. 126.

6. Excerpt from **Nausea, (La Nausée)**, cited in Waelhens, **op. cit.,** p. 368.

7. **Op. cit.**, Gilbert, Stuart, tr. (New York: Modern Library).

8. Job 19:25-27; Psalms 16, 49, 73.

9. J. Leveque, **Job et son Dieu, Essai d'exégèse et de théologie biblique,** Paris, 1970, II, p. 496.

10. **Ibid.**, p. 497.

CHAPTER II

HOPE, AN ENDURING REALITY

In the face of crises and challenges, Christian hope has the power to hold firm. In the words of Saint Paul, it "lasts" (cf. 1 Cor 13:13, etc.). Let us first consider the general fact that hope has held fast and developed to the present in the Church with remarkable continuity. Other hopes have been born, and then disappeared. In our own day, powerful hopes, like that of the Marxists which is the rival of Christian hope, have been in existence for a much shorter time. They are linked to a historical situation and to social structures, and hence seem destined to wear themselves out, to be destroyed or modified as changes come about in the conditions which elicited them.

From certain points of view Christian hope might appear much less firmly rooted, more fragile, because it does not address itself to visible and immediate interests and because spiritual aspirations make much less noise. Nevertheless, Christian hope has resisted every assault upon it, as has the Church itself. It has never stopped growing, while becoming more self-conscious and resolute. Its present crisis will probably simply spur it to greater heights. Indeed, in the image of the Church, Christian hope progresses in and through trials.

However, we cannot limit ourselves to this external appraisal. We must consider hope in depth, to discover its meaning and grasp the ultimate reason why it persists victoriously through all vicissitudes. Hope does not develop on the surface of human emotions and sentiments. It is a profound mode of being that influences the whole of human behavior. We must therefore seek the real power of Christian hope in the recesses of Christian being.

More Than A Virtue

In the categories of traditional theology, hope holds the rank of a virtue. It stands, between faith and love, among the theological virtues, that is to say, among the virtues whose object is God himself. The enumeration of these three virtues is based on Paul's declaration: "There are in the end three things that last: faith, hope, and love, and the greatest of these is love" (I Cor 13:13).[1]

To say that hope is theological is an affirmation of the highest importance, to which we shall return. To hope, in the religious and Christian sense in which we use this word, is to hope in God, and more fundamentally still, to hope for God. Hope involves immediate contact with God, the most intimate fellowship with him. The "death of God" would signify the death of hope. To want to secularize hope by considering it as a relationship with mankind and the world, independently of any direct reference to God, would be to rob it of its most essential element.

That hope is a virtue is evident. Yet in the tradition of the first centuries, faith, hope, and love were considered not strictly as virtues, but rather as principles of the virtues.[2] It was not until the 6th century that Saint Gregory the Great, in his efforts to stress the moral dimension of the Christian life, applied the name "virtue" to the triad: faith, hope, and love.

In commenting on the Scriptural text which attributes seven sons and three daughters to Job, Gregory identifies the sons with the seven virtues of the Holy Spirit and three sisters with the virtues of faith, hope, and love.[3] These three remained alive in the eyes of God when disaster engulfed the entire family in death.[4] We can appreciate this desire to stress the eminent value of faith, hope, and love. There are those who have embellished Saint Gregory's interpretation by calling the three sisters the three most beautiful women in the whole world.[5] This Book of the Old Testament, of course, challenges hope with the problem of the suffering of the innocent. We may therefore be pleased with the presentation of hope as one of Job's daughters, and still wonder whether hope is not a bit constrained in the clothing of a virtue.

Yet it is in such clothing that hope is presented to us by Scholastic theology. In the **Summa Theologiae,** Saint Thomas begins his treatise on hope with the question: "Is hope a virtue?" He answers, relying on the Aristotelian notion of virtue, and concludes that in this instance it is confirmed: hope perfects the one who possesses it and makes his acts good.[6]

The affirmation is irrefutable, but does it fully satisfy us? It would appear to stress a moralism that considers man too exclusively from the point of view of conformity to the good, and evaluates all things in terms of their contribution to the individual's perfection. To define hope as a virtue is to stress the moral attitude and sense the obligation it implies, as well as the merit accruing to the person adopting such an attitude and the good he will obtain from it. In our view, we should look first of all at the interior being of the Christian, seeing hope as one of its basic elements.

Precisely by reason of the fact that hope is theological, it is more than a virtue. Being a direct relationship with God, it is rooted in the divine being. Hope makes man's being share in the divine, profoundly transforming him. The first problem regarding hope is not whether it conforms to the good of the individual, but how to explain it as a fundamental element of Christian being in the plan of salvation and in the communication of divine life.

Moreover, Paul does not speak of three virtues. We cannot even paraphrase his text by saying that "for the present, three virtues that seem inseparable subsist together: Faith, Hope, and Love."[7] The Scriptural text does not say "three virtues," but "three things," according to the Greek. These are three realities, and Paul sees them as divine gifts, charisms, rather than virtues. In fact, he is simply elaborating his earlier advice: "Set your hearts on greater gifts" (1 Cor 12:31). Hope is therefore a charism, a divine gift that enters into the marrow of Christian life.

Now we can better understand the role of hope in Christian being. Paul does not conceive of hope as a way of fulfilling oneself, an attitude that determines a man's decisions concerning his inner being. Hope becomes part and parcel of man's being, but it still comes to him from above. It is of the essence of hope to be received because it is first of all a divine gift.

That is why hope must always be lived as a gift. In response to Scripture's invitations, the Christian might have said: "Let us begin to hope; let us strive to maintain and increase our hope." Instead, the response to the divine call to hope is an attitude of receptiveness: "Let us open ourselves to the hope that is given to us; let us accept this gift more fully." Such an attitude does not obviate human effort. On the contrary, it stimulates it as openness to God's gift. The Christian becomes more completely Christian in the measure that he allows himself to be permeated by hope.

Hope takes hold of us the way God himself does. It is not only a gift, but also a charism of strength. Hope is spiritual energy deployed in us by the Holy Spirit. The spiritual intoxication, somewhat analogous to physical drunkenness, that overcame the disciples on the day of Pentecost (cf. Ac 2:13) abounded with hope. We know this inebriation was fruitful, that it inspired the disciples to indefatigable effort in the service of the kingdom. The person motivated by Christian hope is capable of immense efforts to attain his goals.

A Rope Stretched Taut

It may be supposed that hope is an attitude of soul that passes away.

This might be suggested first of all by the multitude of hopes that stir in the human heart and then vanish. All desires are accompanied by the hope of fulfillment, and for that reason every man's life is crowded with hopes, hopes satisfied and hopes that have failed to materialize. However, the Christian hope of which we speak is not to be confused with the many hopes that come and go in a lifetime. We are talking here about the hope par excellence that governs the totality of a Christian's life.

Even so, hope might be considered to be a transitory attitude. No one can deny it is a bridge between the present and the future. As the temporal dimension of faith, it might seem fated to slip away and disappear when the future invades the present.

We would get the same impression from the image at the source of the Hebrew word **tiqwâh,** which signifies hope: a rope stretched taut.[8] The person who hopes strains toward a goal to be attained. Dissatisfied with the present state of things, he is deeply aware of what he lacks and looks eagerly to the future.

The image is suggestive. It points to the dynamism of the person who is not content to wait passively, but strains toward the goal of his aspirations. Tension implies a mobilization of all one's powers toward the end in view. Hope involves the personality in an attitude most favorable to the attainment of one's goal.

This is not to say that tension needs to be feverish or anxious. It can remain peaceable and serene, and still stimulate human effort.

When we strain forward we are able to exceed what we ordinarily are, and discover within ourselves resources of which we knew nothing. The image invokes a leap that goes far beyond expected capacities. We have many examples and symbols of such leaps in athletic competitions.

To define hope as an athletic attitude of the spiritual order brings out one of its most characteristic aspects.

Hope gives a certain resiliency to human existence; it impels us forward. By contrast, despair can be compared to a broken spring. The person who hopes presses toward the future with an energy that carries him ever onward. He reacts to obstacles with all the more vigor as the rope is stretched tauter.

The image of the taut rope might seem to imply the passing nature of hope. Yet this image cannot express the whole reality. We must turn to Paul's doctrine to better grasp the permanence of hope.

All that we have said about the permanence of hope in no way diminishes its dynamism. Christian hope is a straining toward God that takes powerful hold of a human being and maintains him in a dynamic state that cannot wear itself out.

Hope, A Reality That Lasts

Together with faith and love, hope "lasts." The verb that Paul uses needs careful study, as it has been the subject of many exegetical discussions.

First of all, the word "to last" signifies a permanence

in being, and hence agrees with the fundamental principle that hope is a quality or dimension of Christian being. It even reinforces this affirmation by signifying a being that lasts. The Christian has not only received hope, but continues permanently in hope.

It would not suffice to say the verb "to last" means "to retain validity." That would be as though Paul had declared that only faith, hope and love matter, or that the formula "faith, hope, love, the three inseparable" is valid for the present time.[9] For Paul gives the verb "to last" its fullest meaning here. It is not only a question of validity but of what is, and more precisely of a reality that lasts. The value of this reality lies precisely in its permanence.

The exegetical debate around the word "to last" helps us to penetrate deeper into the more specific problem of hope. It can be stated in this way: Are we to understand Paul's affirmation to mean faith, hope, and love will endure into eternal life, or must we limit the meaning to their permanence during the present life?

Reading the Pauline text, we might think that "to last" signifies an eschatological permanence that extends to the world beyond, for Paul wants to show that love will never pass away, and is not one of those "partial" realities characteristic of the present life.[10] Those who hold to this interpretation usually give the word "now" a purely logical meaning: "in short," "however." This would oblige us to say that hope will endure in the life of the future. But that is to contradict what Paul says elsewhere, when he unequivocally contrasts hope to vision. "How is it possible for one to hope for what he sees?" (Rom 8:24). Faith also appears to be incompatible with vision: "We walk by faith, not by sight" (2 Cor 5:7).

We have to accept this evidence. Faith and hope cannot continue in the life to come as they are now. Hope in particular implies an aspect of expectation, a certain in-

certitude. When the awaited event has occurred, one can
no longer speak of hope in the strict sense in relation to
this event. Paul was aware of the opposition between
hope and vision, and could not have meant to say that
hope persists in the future life.

So hope endures in the present, "now." This temporal
signification must be accepted, because Paul placed himself in a temporal perspective. He contrasted the today
of imperfect knowledge with the more distant moment
of perfect and reciprocal knowledge in immortality.
"Now," as he uses the word, means "during this present
time."

And yet if faith and hope last only during the present
life, are they not as transitory as the other charisms?
Certain exegetes have been inclined to depreciate the
term "to last." For them it means only that during earthly life faith, hope and love "exist together," that is to say,
are inseparable. The words "the greatest of these is love"
(I Cor 13:13) have been interpreted to mean that only
love lasts. In other words, faith and hope will "cease to
be," but only one of the three will subsist "in the end"
because it is the greatest.[11]

Now even while Paul proclaims that love belongs to
a superior order, he places faith and hope on the same
level of excellence with regard to their permanence during the present life. It is of the nature of the three noblest
charisms to "last," and hence the term must have its full
force for faith and hope as well as for love.

The maximum value of the term "to last" is assured
only if it is seen to have eschatological significance, not
for the world beyond but for the "now." In Paul's thinking, to last means to last permanently. In the words of
one commentator, "faith, hope, and love endure forever,
and that includes the present moment . . . Through them
we are even now rooted in the immutability of the world
to come."[12] Absolute permanence characterizes "the

eschatology that has been realized," i.e., the events of the last days that have been accomplished, through Christ, in the today of history and fixed man's new destiny once and for all. Therefore, to last means to possess the duration granted the new man who is being formed in Christ.

Yet, when we affirm this permanent duration are we not claiming that hope persists in the world beyond, whereas Paul, as we have already noted, contrasts hope to vision? In fact, "to last" signifies that the profound, hidden substance of hope is acquired once and for all, and that hope thus culminates in the full possession of what is hoped. Hope ceases to exist in its temporary aspect of imperfection, of uncertain expectation, at the moment the Christian enters the world of eternity, but everything positive hope contained before persists forever. Whatever elements were opposed to vision disappear, but whatever was already an anticipation of the vision retains its reality.

The same holds true of faith, which preserves in the life beyond its substantial reality as a cleaving to God and to Christ. It loses only its veil of obscurity. This is true likewise of love, which, after death, is stripped of all the imperfections and limitations of earthly life, but subsists in its full essence as a gift to God and to neighbor.

Thus, hope contains a reality that does not pass away. To hope is to be permanently established in a state that will last; it is to construct an eternal destiny.

Hope Shares in the Mystery of God's Being

Hope endures, like faith and love. But in the case of hope, this permanence is more surprising. For by definition hope would seem destined to disappear, since it is the expectation of what is to come. Hope exists only as a relationship between the present and the future, and the actualization of the future would appear to put an end to this relationship.

Faith and love are not based on a temporal dimension, and that is why it is much easier to understand how they can last. Faith is the cleaving of the mind and heart to God. The two elements inseparably involved are the affirmation of truth and trust in the One who reveals himself. These are not limited to the present life, but seem destined to last forever. Nor does love involve any temporal limitation. The love that is directed to God and neighbor tends rather to exclude any limitations and aspire to totality and permanence. Hope, on the contrary, is essentially directed toward a final moment in duration. It is totally polarized toward a point in the future, a point that would seem to be its ultimate limit. It is all the more paradoxical, therefore, to claim that hope endures forever.

These considerations spur us to delve even more deeply into the meaning of the words "to last." The point in the future toward which hope tends is a point where eternity and time meet. The object of hope is eternal life for mankind, a life beyond the temporal moment of death and liberated from the limitations of earthly time. If hope were merely a temporal expectation of an eternity to come, it would be deemed to disappear with the advent of this eternity. It would contain only a fragile, continually consumed temporal duration, powerless to subsist in the world beyond. Then hope would leave behind only a passing memory.

If hope lasts it is because it contains something beyond a temporal duration that will pass and disappear. The encounter between eternity and time occurs at the inception of hope, and not only at its term. From the beginning, hope implies an eternal life that has already begun to stir. While this eternal life cannot expect to reach its ultimate stage of development during a man's earthly life, it is already here and now a life of eternity, a life that "lasts."

It is a distinctive mark of God's Being that it lasts.[13] In the Bible, the stability of God is often opposed to the fickleness and instability of creatures. Whereas men are impelled to fluctuations both by their ever-changing being and by their actions that lack constancy and fidelity, God always remains identical to himself.

Hope lasts because it is a participation in the eternal Being of God. To hope is not only to await God's coming and emergence into eternity after death, it is already to live after the manner of God here and now. To hope is to exist in a human way while sharing in God's life. It is to live a mortal life with the mark of eternity on it, and thus possess in advance the goal of this life. As it awaits the final outcome, hope holds the mysterious future in its hands in an obscure and hidden way. Hope is not on the threshold of eternity. It has entered eternity, for it has already taken the decisive step.

It would be better to speak of a mystery rather than a paradox when we describe the hope that lasts. Hope is filled to overflowing with the mystery of divine eternity imbricated in human time.

This amounts to saying that there is a superabundance in the mystery of Christian being. The abyss it reveals is not the abyss of nothingness, but the abyss of eternity, of infinite duration. Whereas certain existentialist philosophers have decried the irremediable emptiness of human existence, we see it as a plenitude of hidden but vitally active being. God has entered into the temporal vessel that is man and into his aspirations for the absolute, making his own eternal life spring up within the depths of man.

The Value of the Here and Now

No less meaningful than the term "to last" is the term "now." Hope endures now, that is to say, it relates to the present life of man.

We would be sadly mistaken to see hope as a flight from the present life, an obsession with a better life beyond. Such a flight from the present would be only a travesty of hope. It would mean that in the face of life's disappointments, in the face of seemingly insurmountable obstacles and trials whose end is out of sight, we would seek refuge in dreams of a happy life after death that will compensate for all we have missed on earth. It would imply a negative, pessimistic judgment on the present state of mankind, a refusal to strive to make the world better, a scepticism as to the value of efforts to help the human community advance morally and spiritually.

This temptation is all the more dangerous for the Christian because it may seem to be founded on very lofty views, on the exclusive desire for the good things of the world beyond. We know that Christian spirituality has not always escaped this danger. In some of the old liturgy's petitions for the grace to scorn earthly things and aspire solely for the blessings of heaven, we can discern the danger of camouflaging escape as a sublime hope.

Even in our own time, this temptation persists. Obviously, the tendency today is probably to emphasize the importance of earthly values, as well as the urgency of collaborating in their attainment. Yet in the face of excesses in this direction, there is the continued danger of over-reacting in the opposite direction. This would consist in clinging to heavenly values, while backing away from any commitment to share in the urgent tasks of the here and now. When we try to escape from our world as it is, we are rejecting its demands and conditions and consequently refusing to play the part in it to which we have been called. This amounts to a negation of hope.

Far from despising the "now," authentic hope acknowledges its value and reality. Through hope, this "now" becomes not simply a moment in time that quickly passes, but eternal life begun. Our "now" thus acquires a new density of meaning, the density of eternity.[14]

Here again we see the paradox of hope. It is the expectation of a better future and might thus seem to imply a depreciation of the present. Actually, the reverse is true. Hope tends to increase and restore the value of earthly existence with each passing moment, to give it an added dimension. The reason for this is that eternal happiness can only be prepared in our todays. Therefore every minute is precious because it enables eternal life to become more firmly rooted in mankind. It is rich with possibilities for the building up of the life to come. The immutable world of the future is constructed within the ever-changing time of human life. Each present moment carries within it the seeds of eternity.

Let us grasp the meaning of this valorization of the "now." In no sense does it attribute to earthly time an absolute value of its own, after the manner of those who seek in life's ephemeral joys the absolute and the eternity they cannot give. It increases the value of the "now" because of the divine life that transforms it and raises it to the level of a permanent duration. The absolute and the eternal hidden within this superior life make it possible for us to live our mortal lives, as it were, above time.

Instead of deluding itself as to the flimsiness of time and the fluctuations of man's earthly life, this view frankly acknowledges them. It accepts the disappointments, difficulties, and trials inherent to our present human condition. But it sees in them the temporal path by which the eternity of God takes possession of human life. Plunged in the mystery of the "now," hope rises to a level which is already on the summits of eternal happiness.

"God, The Source of Hope"

The reason hope endures is because God is "the source of hope." This is the way Paul defines God in his Epistle to the Romans: "So may God, the source of hope, fill you with all joy and peace in believing so that through the power of the Holy Spirit you may have hope in abundance" (Rm 15:13).

To grasp the power of Paul's words we must remember the importance the Jews attributed to names, and especially to the name of God. Among all the deities that claimed the homage of men, God had affirmed his identity to the Jews by revealing his name. There was, for instance, the scene in Exodus in which Moses asked the One who was sending him to deliver the Jews from the Egyptian yoke to reveal his name. The Lord's answer was characteristic. He identified himself as "I AM" (Ex 3:14).

The God of Christianity is presented to us as "God, the source of hope." Not only is this his name, but it suffices to distinguish him. The God who revealed himself in Christ is the One who brought hope to the world. This hope is intrinsic to his identity as it has been made known to us. The reason why the Christian can be defined as the man of hope is because he has identified himself as "the source of hope."

False gods have never ceased drawing men's eyes to themselves and seducing their minds. Mankind has certainly gotten beyond the stage when deities fought wars among themselves in every nation. Yet we are still confronted with diverse images of God. God's face can only be the face of hope. An image that would inspire fear above all else could not reveal the real identity of our God. A God who darkened human life instead of brightening and rejoicing it could not be the God who came to us in Jesus. Christian faith can only be faith in the God of hope.

In what sense is God "the source of hope"? The expression might be given diverse meanings: the God for whom we hope, the God in whom our hope rests, the God who inspires hope. Paul's meaning is that God is the author of hope. He makes hope "superabound" within Christians.

God is revealed as the Creator of hope through the salvation he has offered all men in Jesus Christ. Granted, hope is not a thing and cannot be created, strictly speaking. But salvation is the creation of a new man, and this new man is filled with hope. Through his grace, God creates souls that hope.

Not only is God the source of hope, he is also the One for whom we hope, the One in whom we hope. Paul does not seem to have directly addressed himself to these aspects. And yet if we reflect on the way God is the author of hope, we must recognize he is also essentially the object of hope and the reason for our hope.

Actually, God creates hope in men by sharing his own life with them. The substance of Christian hope consists in the communication of divine life. Under the Old Covenant hope was directed to life, to a life of complete fulfillment. It attains this goal in a superior way under the New Covenant. God's life grows in man. That is the ultimate reason why hope "lasts." We have already stressed this: hope is a participation in the eternal Being of God. "To last" signifies the entrance of eternity into the world of time. To live in hope is to live the way God himself lives; it is to dominate the flow of time.

One last question might arise: Is not God, "the source

of hope," likewise a God who hopes? The idea is foreign to Paul's thinking, at least in its explicit formulation. For in Paul's perspective, hope is linked to the imperfection of earthly life that cannot yet see or possess what it hopes for.

Nevertheless, if God is the author of hope and inspires it by giving mankind a part in his divine life, does he not share in the hope he kindles and brings to flower among men? Does he not look toward the future, freely to be sure and not only out of love for men, but with real expectation? Is he not the first to await the final completion of the work of salvation? The answer is that he looks to its coming with far greater desire than we do.

It may be objected that in God there can be no incertitude, which is a mark of human hope. Let us not be too quick to agree. God cannot experience uncertainty concerning his own omnipotence in realizing his plans. However, in the measure that he accepts human liberty, he admits incertitude as to the use of this liberty. He has reason for incertitude only as far as men are concerned. Yet uncertainty has a part in God's plans too, because he respects free human decisions and accepts them through love. Having decreed that the progress of salvation history should depend on men's free choices, God hopes these choices will be favorable to him. He hopes because he has refused to confiscate liberty, and has willed to let it follow its course amid hesitations and retreats.

In this light, it can be said that no hope is stretched so taut as God's. No one is so resolutely turned toward the promise of the future as God is, or so eager to see its rapid and complete realization.

Now we see better that the hope that exists in God is communicated to man as a reality that lasts. For the Christian, to hope is to participate in the immense hope that, in God, accompanies the unfolding of the saga of salvation.

This explains why hope is filled with such certitude. The certitude of the man who hopes stems from the certitude of the One who, in his wisdom, decreed the world's destiny and who, in his omnipotence, infallibly guides it to completion. In the measure that we doubt our power to persevere and are uncertain as to our future course, we receive through hope the divine power that gives us absolute certitude of attaining the final goal of our life. What is asked of us is simply to safeguard within us the certitude that God, "the source of hope," is constantly communicating to us.

NOTES FOR CHAPTER TWO

1. It is rather surprising that Moltmann's work **Théologie de l'espérance** (French translation, Paris, 1970), refrains from commenting upon or even citing this text. This work appeared in English under the title, **Theology of Hope on the Ground and Implications of a Christian Eschatology**, (New York, Harper & Row, 1967).

2. Cf. A. Michel, "Vertu," **Dictionnaire de Théologie Catholique**, Vol. 15, 2746.

3. **Moralia**, I, 38; PL 75, 544 D.

4. **Moralia**, II, 79; PL 75, 594.

5. Cf. Michel, Article, "Vertu," **DTC**, 2747. Actually, this praise of beauty is applied to the three daughters that Job had after his misfortune, (42:15), whereas St. Gregory speaks of the three daughters that Job had before that time, (1:2).

6. II II, Q. 17, a. 1. For a commentary on this passage, cf. C. A. Bernard, **Théologie de l'espérance selon saint Thomas d'Aquin**, Paris, 1961, p. 48.

7. E. B. Allo, **Premiere épître aux Corinthiens**, Paris, 1934, p. 351.

8. To analyze the terms the Old Testament uses to designate hope, cf. J. van der Ploeg, "L'espérance dans l'Ancien Testament," **Revue Biblique** 61, (1954), pp. 481-507.

9. W. Groussouw, "L'espérance dans le Nouveau Testament," **Revue Biblique** 61, (1954), 517. C. Spicq has criticized this interpretation for assuming that the other charisms have no value for the present time, (**Agapè dans le Nouveau Testament, II**, Paris, 1959, p. 108, No. 2).

10. For example, we can cite the following who offer various nuances of interpretation: A. T. Robertson, and A. Plummer, **First Epistle of St. Paul to the Corinthians,** Edinburgh, 1911, admit a constant progress in the state of glory; R. Bultmann, **Le christianisme primitif,** Paris, 1960, p. 152, admits of no definitive state of salvation inasmuch as for him Christian existence consists of faith and hope and thereby tends "toward the grace of God as always in the immediate future." M. F. Lacan, "Les trois qui demeurent," **Recherches de Science Religieuse,** 46, (1958), pp. 321-343, holds that faith and hope have two different meanings, one linked to earthly life and the other to life eternal.

11. Groussouw, art. cit., RB 1954, pp. 517ff.

12. F. Dreyfus, "Maintenant la foi, l'espérance et la charité demeurent toutes les trois, (1 Cor. 13:13)," **Studiorum palinorum congressus internationalis catholicus,** Romae, 1963, p. 411.

13. This fundamental sense of the verb "last" appears clearly in the Old and New Testaments. In discerning this, F. Hauck relates the faith, hope, and love of 1 Cor. 13:13 to "divine things," (**Theologisches Wörterbuch zum Neuen Testament, IV,** p. 579).

14. The Johannine "now" expresses this sense of a contemporary fulfillment of eschatological hopes. But, as H. Stählin notes, John's was not an isolated interpretation. Rather, it was the elaboration of a widely held view within the early Christian community (**Theologisches Wörterbuch zum Neuen Testament, IV,** 1113).

CHAPTER III

THE INCARNATION, MYSTERY OF HOPE

We have spoken of the relations between God and man in hope. We have still to grasp the essential mark of Christian hope, by understanding the role of Christ in all authentic human hope.

As we have noted, the hope of the Jews in the Old Testament was entirely founded on the Covenant. Because of this, their hope was more than the expectation of future fulfillment. It rested on a permanent, ever-present foundation. Through the mystery of the Incarnation, the Covenant assumes ontological density. In the ontological unity of the Person of the Word, God and man have been joined. The foundation of hope can no longer be limited to relations of love, to a divine promise of unceasing help to which human trust responds. Christian hope is founded on a Person in whom are expressed both the promise and its trusting acceptance, the divine gift and the certitude that the deepest human aspirations will be realized.

Christ, Our Hope

The very first lines of the First Epistle to Timothy identify Christ with hope: "Paul, an apostle of Christ Jesus by the command of God our savior and Christ Jesus our hope" (1 Tm 1:1). It is in the most general sense of the term that he is our hope.[1] The parallel with "God our savior" indicates that the salvation God wants to give us is contained in Christ. The reason Paul does not say that God our savior is our hope is because in Christ Jesus we possess the reality of our salvation in a more immediate and concrete way. It is equally remarkable that the apostolic mission is under the command of Christ our hope. Paul is an apostle by his command, and his work is therefore to put to work the hope contained in Christ.

In the Letter to the Colossians, Paul speaks of the "mystery," that is to say, God's plan to be carried out in the evangelization of the pagans. The "mystery hidden from ages and generations past" has now been revealed. "This mystery has been brought to the Gentiles—the mystery of Christ in you, your hope of glory" (Col 1:26-27). Such is the Christ the Apostle Paul preaches: "This is the Christ we proclaim . . . hoping to make every man complete in Christ. For this I work and struggle, impelled by that energy of his which is so powerful a force within me" (Col 1:28-29).

The source of apostolic energy is therefore to be found in Christ, our "hope of glory," and this hope accomplishes the "mystery." This means that our hope is more than the conjunction of all human aspirations. It is true, of course, that Jesus answers these aspirations and that the deepest desires of mankind converge toward him. But by manifesting the "mystery," hope first of all fulfills God's own desire and his omnipotent will. Christ is the hope that God has placed in our very midst.

As Paul emphasizes, it is a hope of special importance for the pagans. Before Christ came it had not yet been granted to them: "Remember that, in former times, you had no part in Christ and were excluded from the community of Israel. You were strangers to the covenant and its promise; you were without hope and without God

in the world" (Ep 2:12). To be without Christ is to be
without hope.

This is the fundamental truth. Not only does Christ
inspire hope, he is hope. The identification enables us to
better understand both what hope is and who Christ is.

Hope is concentrated, fully realized in Christ. From
this point of view, Christ has the role attributed to
Yahweh in the Old Testament. Yahweh had been called
the hope of Israel (Jr 14:8; 17:13). Now Christ is the hope,
and in a more universal way because he is the hope of
the pagans as well. Those who had no hope because they
had no God now find in Christ both God and hope.

Paul speaks of the "hope of glory," thereby indicating
the totally supernatural, heavenly orientation of hope.
Even though we already possess hope since Christ is in
our midst, our hope looks to the world beyond. Its ultimate term is the glory that crowns human destinies after
death, permeating the human with the divine.

Hope identified with Christ is distinct from the Christian's subjective attitude of hope. It is the foundation of
this attitude, what we might call the objective state of
hope, its ontological basis. Christ holds within himself
the whole of mankind's hope, because in him is the source
of man's future development and the final goal to which
man is called. Every man must be made complete in
Christ, to use Paul's expression (cf. Col 1:28). All progress
toward perfection thus starts with Christ and is accomplished in him.

This leads us to still another conclusion. To identify
Christ with hope means not only that all Christian hope
resides in Christ, but also that everything Christ means
for us can be expressed in terms of hope. Hope somehow
sums up here and now the work of salvation accomplished by Christ.

To return to the expression "Christ, the hope of

glory," Christian life must be understood in its entirety as involving an intimate bond between our present state and our future glory, or more exactly as glory already begun and germinally present in our mortal lives.

Christ is therefore the whole of our present and future, as well as our future contained in our present. Nothing about the future is foreign to him. As the dispenser of glory for all mankind, he possesses within himself the final goal of earthly time.

Thus, everything that comes to us from Christ must be in the nature of hope. In the measure that our lives are quickened by his, we live in "the hope of glory."

The Prelude to Hope in the Eternity of the Word

The mystery of the Incarnation turned the temporal dimension of human life topsy-turvy. It introduced divine eternity into the heart of human time. Henceforth time, contained within eternity, would be orientated toward a term far superior to itself, a term whose substance it already possessed in principle.

The advent of eternity into time is especially emphasized in the Prologue to Saint John's Gospel. But it already crops up in the Synoptics when they point to a hope that came down from above at the origin of Jesus' earthly life. Mark's laconic reference is indicative of this: "Here begins the gospel of Jesus Christ, the Son of God" (Mk 1:1). The "Good News" or "Gospel" signifies a message of hope, brought to us by the "Son of God." Luke and Matthew show how the child whose name announced his mission as Savior was conceived by the work of the Holy Spirit. At the origin of Jesus and of the hope that comes to us through him, we encounter a divine mystery.

What remained implicit in the Synoptics was made explicit in the Fourth Gospel. John chose to begin his Gospel not with temporality but with eternity. For that was the real beginning that preceded the Creation recorded in Genesis. "In the beginning was the Word." We cannot understand Christ if we do not turn back to this absolute beginning. The Word was in eternity, in divine eternity in the strict and absolute sense. "The Word was God."

In this eternity there was dynamic activity: "The Word was in God's presence," or to put it more exactly, "toward" God, that is to say, "toward" the Father. The Word was continually turning toward the Father. The sentence has often been translated: "The Word was with God," as the Latin version of the Vulgate had already interpreted it. However, current exegesis tends to acknowledge the dynamic value of the Greek preposition "toward" (pros).[2]

From all eternity the dynamism of the Word impelled him toward the Father. Here we see the origin of the first announcement of hope. There was prefigured in the gaze of the Son turned toward the Father the gaze that mankind would some day turn in the same direction.[3]

The meaning of the preposition pros, whose use we have already noted, is that this gaze was somehow the first prospect of a future that would lead the whole of creation toward the Father. Strictly speaking, we cannot say that the Word's first gaze was the gaze of hope, but we must affirm that the movement and the polarization that orientated the entire Being of the Son toward the Father were the bases of the dynamism that would later quicken human hope.

From the human point of view, the primordial origin of hope resides, as we have already noted, in man's fundamental need for God, the keenly sensed need of every human mind under the influence of grace. Man is starving for God. But there is a divine origin to hope in the Son's need of the Father, in his eternal turning toward the Father.

The first rope stretched taut, so to speak, is the Word, reaching out to the Father with all the force of eternity. And that explains why, in hope, permanence and polarization are not in opposition.

Besides, if man becomes aware of his need for God through the operation of grace, it is because, in this very awareness, he shares the Son's aspiration toward the Father. Hope is formed by a filial movement that seeks the greatest possible fellowship with the One in whom it discovers a Father's love.

The Virgin Birth

The influx of eternity into time came about through the virgin birth. When Saint John was about to affirm that the Word became flesh, he affirmed with visible insistence the virginal character of a birth whose only source was God himself: "begotten not by blood, nor by carnal desire, nor by man's willing it, but by God" (Jn 1:13).[4]

The virginal conception was the human manifestation of divine sonship, especially in view of the fact that in the Johannine text it is linked to the gift granted to believers of becoming children of God. Before John, Luke had already thrown light on the link between Jesus' divine sonship and his miraculous conception: "The Holy Spirit will come upon you and the power of the Most High will overshadow you; hence, the holy offspring to be born will be called Son of God" (Lk 1:35).

In meditating on this fundamental fact, John saw more clearly revealed the identity of the eternal Word turned toward the Father and become man to live as one of us. And in this singular and exceptional mode of birth he discerned a universal hope. The generation accomplished by the Holy Spirit inaugurated a new humanity whose living principle was no longer blood or man's will, but God himself.

This time, there was question of a hope in the strict sense, for it was implanted in a human nature and introduced into the history of humanity as a new mutational seed. When the Word became incarnate through the virginal conception, his divine sonship became the wellspring of divine sonship within the human community. He communicated a truly divine power, the power that is the mark of the child of God.[5]

Now the significance of Jesus' virginal birth is clearly apparent in the formation of hope. Among all the events that make up a human life, birth takes a pre-eminent place as the announcement of a new future. One might say that being born is the superlative hope-event, not only for the child who comes into the world, but also his parents and for all who surround him. When a child is born he tends to renew the climate into which he comes and to rejuvenate those around him who are many years his senior. He brings a new life and appears endowed with inexhaustible potential.

The virginal birth brought newness of life in the maximum degree, and thereby raised the quality and scope of hope as well.

Negatively, the virgin birth was a rupture with the normal order of human generations, in which the present is determined by the past inasmuch as each child is the product of two heredities. The virginal character of Jesus' conception removed him from this hereditary determinism. It liberated him from the all-powerful tyranny of the past, and opened an entirely different future to him.

Positively, the virgin birth resulted from the conjunction of the divine Fatherhood and a human motherhood. It introduced an entirely new wellspring of life, far superior to any human powers of generation. The virgin birth transformed what in an ordinary birth would have been merely undefined and uncertain potentialities into an infinite potential for development. When the Son of God was born of the Father by the action of the Holy Spirit into the world of time, he opened up a limitless future for human life. He laid the foundations of a hope that exceeds all human aspirations. He brought with him the freshness that springs from God's eternal youth and has the power to perpetually rejuvenate the human community.

The unique fact of Jesus' virginal birth throws light on the subsequent flowering of the state of virginity in the Church. Virginity voluntarily adopted is truly the boldest of hopes. It is the hope of a spiritual fruitfulness in the kingdom of God, a hope that renounces the human means of multiplying life and chooses to expect from God's power the formation and diffusion of a superior life throughout mankind.

Woman and Hope

The virgin birth invites us to reflect on the link that exists between womanhood and hope. This involves an important truth that might be overlooked when we affirm that all hope centers in Christ. Does not such an affirmation identify hope with a man, and hence pose the question why woman is excluded?

To see this question in the light of the message of Revelation, let us remember that according to the biblical account of the creation, the Creator placed the entire hope of humankind in a couple: "Be fertile and multiply; fill the earth and subdue it" (Gn 1:28). Why, then, should we expect supernatural hope to rest solely on man, without woman's cooperation?

The mystery of the Incarnation clearly implies such cooperation. While, objectively speaking, the hope of the human race rests on Christ, we must add that, subjectively speaking, woman's hope was required for the formation of Christ and the accomplishment of his work. It is all set forth in the account of the Annunciation.

The first thing the angel's message demanded of Mary, if she was to consent to the virginal motherhood offered her, was faith. But it also called for hope on her part, since it announced the child's Messianic future. If Mary was to cooperate in the realization of this future, she would need hope, a long-range and unwavering hope. So we see that in the covenant God made with the human race, woman's hope was to play a very special role.

The hope called for was specifically feminine, the hope of a mother who expects everything of her child. Every mother tends to indulge in boundless hope as she dreams of her child's future. In Mary's case the light of hope had a solid, unshakeable foundation, namely, God's plan that would infallibly be realized. The Gospel text promises perpetual duration to the reign of the son of David: "and his reign will be without end" (Lk 1:33). Mary's hope was thus offered a perspective of eternal dimensions.

In addition, by reason of her motherhood, Mary's hope was more than acceptance of God's word. She already possessed in a hidden and secret but very real way what she desired. From the moment of the virginal conception, Mary was inhabited by a presence. The salvation of humanity was no longer a remote goal. It was entirely contained within the child "God saves." This confirmed the characteristic mark of Christian hope, which is founded not on a mere announcement but on an actual realization.

The man who summed up the hope of the world's liberation was thus received within a woman's womb through hope. It was within a woman that hope passed from its Jewish form to its Christian form and became hope in Jesus.

Besides, during Jesus' years at Nazareth, Mary's hope must have continued to grow. As evidence of this we have Mary's request at the marriage feast of Cana. She asked for a miracle, revealing an immense hope in her Son's divine power and the expectation that he would manifest his role as Savior. In the context of Cana, woman's cooperation with man in the work of salvation has special meaning. It can be defined as the initiative of woman's hope, impatient to obtain what it desires.

Then too, motherhood itself is extremely suggestive of hope. From conception to birth, a quiet, secret development occurs that culminates in the emergence of a life into the light. From this point of view, woman seems predestined to live hope, to keep it hidden within her with the certitude of a luminous outcome.

The link between womanhood and hope could be confirmed by citing countless instances in which a woman's hope has inspired and sustained a man's course of action. Men who might have been inclined to limit themselves to more modest goals have been impelled to develop their talents and use all their resources through the influence of a woman's ambition. Regardless of the direction it takes, a woman's ambition has remarkable power and exercises great influence.

This psychological fact helps us to understand the role woman's hope has played in the work of salvation. The primordial importance of Mary's hope in the mystery of the Incarnation explains the importance of woman's hope in the present-day mystery of the Church.

This womanly hope can take on various forms. As a perpetuation of Mary's hope, it may assume a virginal form, completely dedicated to the spiritual expansion of the kingdom of Christ. It can even be said that in this case the theocentric character of hope is verified still more. Virginity cannot be understood in a purely negative way, as simply a renouncement. It is ordered toward a motherhood of a higher and more universal order, and is therefore a stronger hope.

Other forms of feminine hope are more common. The wife who establishes a home and the mother who raises her children bring to the Church the hope of a community of love and of new, more abundant Christian lives. Then, there are many women who live celibate lives as a result of circumstances they have not chosen. Is not this celibacy an invitation to a more lively hope in the Lord? Seen in the light of faith, it appears to reveal a mysterious call to a more hidden fruitfulness, and a more generous concern for neighbor, for the spiritual enrichment of the Church and of the world.

It is evident, therefore, that physical motherhood is not the only condition that involves woman in the path of hope. Christ used the image of the pain and joy of a woman in childbirth to define the participation of all disciples, whether men or women, in the drama of Redemption and to situate this participation in the context of hope. The image applies to everyone, but the fact that it is based on woman's role helps to show the intimate relationship between woman and hope.

The Word Enters the World of Human Becoming

The verb "become" that John uses to describe the progress of the Incarnation is singularly important, because it stresses the transition from the stability of eternal being to the change inherent in becoming: "The Word became flesh" (Jn 1:14). From the start, the Prologue expresses the opposition between divine Being and the becoming of creation. "In the beginning was the

Word," and "through him all things came into being" (Jn 1:1-3). The amazing thing about the action of the Word stems from the fact that even though he continued in eternal being, he chose to share the becoming of creatures. The One through whom "all things came into being" accepted the becoming he had fashioned for others, and assumed this inferior mode of existence.

Now, when Jesus entered the world of becoming, he transformed it. He brought to becoming an incomparably richer fabric of being, for in the act of becoming flesh he continued to be God, eternal. His eternity carried his human becoming within itself, without stripping it of its specific nature of mutability.

The Incarnation, therefore, established a new relationship between eternity and time that implanted hope within human becoming. All that has been said earlier about hope's participation in eternal being must be understood in the light of the mystery of the Incarnation. For it was through this mystery that divine Being entered the world of time and set up an unchanging, permanent abode within it.

It is only when becoming remains imprisoned within itself that it begets despair. To prove it we have the laments on the flight of time and the brevity of life, as well as the lyricism of the poets about a love that yearns to be eternal but cannot overcome the ravages of time. These bear witness to the disillusionment of a becoming which makes mortal man feel he is being swept away.

Man has the sensation that the earth is giving way beneath his feet, that passing moments of time vanish one after the other, leaving him nothing solid to hold on to.

The Incarnation opened man's becoming to the gift of being. In so doing it brought hope within the human horizon, rooting and "ontologizing" hope in being. As a result of the Incarnation time is now more than a present moment constantly being consumed, and man's polarization toward the future has superior meaning.

Jesus had the certitude that his being could not be engulfed in the bottomless abyss of becoming. His affirmation "I am" resounds with singular power. This was the first time a man could claim as his own the name claimed by God himself in the Old Testament. To say, as did the God of Sinai, "I AM" (Ex 3:14) or like the God of the second Isaiah "It is I" (Is 43:10),[6] in the sense of an I that enjoys immutable being,[7] is to make an extremely bold assertion. And yet this assertion expressed what Christ realized himself to be.[8]

A Johannine text stresses the opposition between being and becoming: "Before Abraham came to be, I AM" (Jn 8:58). Abraham came into existence, he "became," whereas the "I am" had been present from all eternity.[9] With these words Jesus revealed he knew he dominated the becoming that had preceded him. The history of the Jewish people finds its meaning in him. He holds within himself the whole of hope. From the beginning, hope pointed toward him: "Your father Abraham rejoiced that he might see my day. He saw it and was glad" (Jn 8:56). At a deeper level, the becoming of the chosen people was already mysteriously sustained by the "I am" of Christ. This "I am" was not merely a final term, the fulfillment of a promise; it was a hidden involvement in this becoming, a secret principle that impelled its development.

The purpose of such affirmations as "I am" or "it is I" was to kindle hope. This had already been true of the revelation of God's name in Exodus, in which the Lord said: "I am who am," so as to give Moses the guarantee of a firm and unshakable covenant: "I will be with you" (Ex 3:14,12). We should reread the declarations in which Jesus applied this divine name to himself. It will be apparent that they were made with the same end in mind: to give a definitive basis for hope.

Chapter 8 of John's Gospel, in which the expression recurs three times, is filled with the announcement of a superior future toward which Jesus was proceeding and that would manifest his "I am." "When you lift up the Son of Man, you will come to realize that I AM" (Jn 8:28). In Chapter 13, hope sees in the "I am" the certitude of overcoming trials: "I tell you this now, before it takes place, so that when it takes place you may believe that I AM" (Jn 13:19).

In the dialogue with the Samaritan woman, Jesus' "I am he" (cf. Jn 4:26), amounted to proclaiming that all the hope of those who await the Messiah is realized in him. When Jesus walked on the water, his "It is I" (Jn 6:20; Mt 14:27; Mk 6:50) was intended to give the disciples the assurance that in all the troubled crossings of their boat they would enjoy the pacifying presence that would make them overcome all difficulties. At the moment of the Passion, Jesus' "I am he" (Jn 18:5, 6, 8) addressed to those who had come to arrest him,[10] and especially the "I am" of his response to Caiphas (Mk 14:62; Lk 22:70), indicated a presence that could never be obliterated from this earth, even by death.

Complete assurance regarding the future is thus found in a present rich with eternity. Jesus did not even have to speak in the future tense to give a basis for hope. The present "I am" sufficed. That is why the substance of Christian hope is contained in the present.

The Return to The Father

The action of the Word who became flesh involved not only the movement of the Son begotten of the Father by way of human generation, but also the movement of the Son's return to the Father.

How does the Prologue define the work of revelation

accomplished in the Incarnation? "For while the law was given through Moses, this enduring love came through Jesus Christ. No one has ever seen God. It is God the only Son, ever at the Father's side, who has revealed him" (Jn 1:17-18). The law was given and transmitted through Moses. As for the truth, it was not simply given, but accomplished. Literally, it "became." Just as the eternal Word became flesh, so eternal truth entered into the process of becoming.

This truth is essentially the truth of God. Through the Incarnation, the only Son has made this truth known to us. He "revealed" God, because being turned toward the Father's heart he penetrated to the depths of the divine mystery.[11]

The work of revelation therefore consists in making us enter "into the Father's bosom" through our sight.

To see God is a supreme goal of human hope, since the beatitude of eternity has been shown to consist in this vision. As Saint John says: "No one has ever seen God" (1 Jn 4:12). Now, although this vision is impossible to man left to his own resources, in Christ it becomes possible in a certain measure. The Word made flesh has made us know what he himself has intimately experienced.

Philip said to Jesus: "Lord, show us the Father and that will be enough for us." In response Jesus made him understand that his great aspiration to see the Father had already been satisfied: "Philip, after I have been with you all this time, you still do not know me? Whoever has seen me has seen the Father. How can you say, 'Show us the Father?' Do you not believe that I am in the Father and the Father is in me?" (Jn 14:8-10).

When Jesus said "Whoever has seen me has seen the Father," he did not give the word "see" the full meaning it has when it designates the heavenly vision of God. Philip's question had been asked in the context of earthly life. He wanted to see the Father then and there. And so the word "see" could not have meant the intuitive vision without any intermediary, which is the mark of heavenly beatitude.

In any event, Philip had in mind a spiritual knowledge with a certain intuitive element. Christ had let his disciples see him in an intimate contact that revealed the nature of God to them in a direct and vital way. Insofar as earthly vision permitted, this intuitive contact with God inaugurated the contact of the beatific vision. It contained everything leading to this vision that was compatible with the conditions of mortal life. When the verb "see" is used in the Gospel, we must give it a certain weight of authentic vision, albeit short of the splendor of the ultimate vision of heaven.

The only man ever to see God is Jesus, who as the Word is eternally turned toward the Father's heart. And this deep knowledge he shared with his disciples. More specifically, he made them glimpse the Father by revealing himself, by making known what it means to be the Person of the Son.

All hope of the vision of God therefore rests in Christ. Actually, the word "vision" is too narrow because it concerns only the aspect of revelation. Now, Christ was turned toward the Father not only to know him and make him known, but also to be united to him in total mutual love. Having come from the Father, he was going to the Father and to their eternal fellowship, and he was fully aware of it (Jn 13:1-3). He was going to prepare a place for his disciples at his Father's side. He wanted to draw them after him in his progression toward the Father. In this broader role, he was the hope of all men whom he was leading to the Father not only that they might know the Father but for total union with him.

This return to the Father was completed in the Paschal mystery which consummated the work of the Incarnation.

NOTES FOR CHAPTER THREE

1. C. Spicq points in particular to the parallel with Tt. 1:2, so as not to limit the expression to the expectation of the Parousia. "Christ is the mainstay or foundation of the hope for eternal life," (Les épitres pastorales, I, Paris, 1969, p. 316).

2. Cf. I. de Potterie, "L'emploi de eis dans S. Jean et ses incidences théologiques, **Biblica** 43, (1962), pp. 379-387; "Je suis la voie, la vérité, la vie", (Jn. 14:6), **Nouvelle Revue Théologique**, 88, (1966), 934; A. Feuillet, **Le prologue du quatrième é vangile**, Paris, 1968, pp. 264-269.

3. This perspective appears later, in verse 18 where the only Son, turned "toward the Father's bosom," ["ever at the Father's side," **New American Bible**], tells us what manner of Being God is. Here again the **eis** which indicates a movement has been interpreted by certain exegetes as equivalent to an immobile "in." Calling to mind Hellenistic usage, C. K. Barrett cites Acts 2:5, which speaks of a large crowd "staying in [eis] Jerusalem" (**The Gospel according to St. John**, London, 1962, p. 141). But there, too, **eis** indicates the movement of those who had come to the city for the celebration of the feast. In John 13:23, the expression "in Jesus' bosom" ["reclined close to him," **N.A.B.**], with the preposition **en**, does not imply movement. The comparison leads us to think that in John 1:18 the preposition **eis** is meant to give a different nuance of meaning, and to imply veritable movement.

4. For the version in the singular and for the interpretation of this verse, cf. our work **Etre né de Dieu, Jean 1, 13**, Rome, 1969.

5. This should be interpreted to mean: "the power that consists in becoming children of God." Cf. M. E. Boismard, **Le prologue de saint Jean**, Paris, p. 62. The power does not precede the granting of divine sonship. Rather, this sonship itself is given as a power.

6. Cf. also Is. 41:4; 43:13; 46:4; 48:12; Dt. 32:39. Cf. Barrett, **St. John**, p. 283, and A. Feuillet, "Les Ego eimi christologiques due quatrième évangile," **Recherches de Science Religieuse, 54**, (1966), pp. 5-22.

7. According to Barrett, op. cit., the expression means the eternal being of Jesus, and thus places Jesus on a par with God.

8. Cf. the present author's work, **La conscience de Jésus**, Gembloux, 1971, pp. 55-75.

9. Barrett paraphrases: Before Abraham came into existence, I existed eternally, as I now am, and shall continue to be forever, (**St. John**, p. 292).

10. C. H. Dodd compares this triple repetition to the one in Jn. 4:50, 51, 53: "Your son will live," to stress that a very natural expression took on particular importance, precisely by virtue of a repetition that was not natural. (**Historical Tradition in the Fourth Gospel**, Cambridge, 1963, p. 75, No. 2). Besides, the "I am he" of the arrest must be considered as one of the marks of sovereignty Jesus manifested on that occasion.

11. Cf. Barrett, **St. John**, p. 141: The verb used here by John, "to reveal," was used in the Hellenistic language in explaining the divine secrets, sometimes by the gods themselves.

CHAPTER IV

REDEMPTION AND HOPE

When Paul speaks of Christ, our "hope of glory" (Col 1:27), he means the glorious Christ. Jesus' earthly life was only a passing phase. The Incarnation could produce all its fruits and become the hope of humanity only through the Paschal mystery. Everything we have said so far about the efficacy of the Incarnation must be understood in the light of the Redemption and its outcome.

If we are to understand hope, we must first reflect on our Savior's death and Resurrection.

Hope attained its full dimensions only when the love involved in the Incarnation mystery was deployed to its utmost limit in sacrifice, and when divine glory took possession of Jesus in his entire human nature.

The Hour

From the first moment, Jesus' coming into the world is presented by Luke (1:31-33) and by Matthew (1:21) as the prelude to a great work. The child was to fulfill Messianic hopes by bringing salvation to men. And so it is not the Incarnation or the birth of the child in themselves that saved mankind and transformed the human condition. What saved the world was the fact that Jesus carried out the Father's decree.

Throughout his earthly life Jesus was the bearer of a hope that would soon be realized. When he entered upon his public mission, he kindled this hope among his hearers. The primary theme of his preaching was this: "The reign of God is at hand!" (Mk 1:15; Mt 3:2). The kingdom had not yet come, but its advent was imminent. This was still the hope of the Old Testament founded on God's promises, and it was now close to fulfillment.

Exactly when would this kingdom come? In John's Gospel there are several references to Jesus' hour, the supreme hour, when his ultimate destiny would be accomplished and a new destiny unfurled for the universe.

The Father himself had decreed that hour. As long as it had not yet rung, Jesus' enemies could not lay hold of him: "At this they tried to seize him, but no one laid a finger on him because his hour had not yet come" (Jn 7:30). Even when he entered the Temple with amazing boldness to disseminate his teaching, making himself vulnerable to his enemies' blows, he remained unscathed. "Still, he went unapprehended, because his hour had not yet come" (Jn 8:20).

These events revealed the Father's omnipotence that dominated the drama of the Passion. Neither chance accidents nor human intrigues could destroy Jesus' life. When Jesus' death on the cross is described as the confrontation between his enemies' relentless hatred and his equally persevering fidelity, we do not yet touch the primary source of the event, namely, the Father's mysterious decree. In his anguish before the tragic prospect that faced him, Jesus addressed himself to the Father because he knew everything depended on him: "My soul is troubled now, yet what should I say—Father, save me from this hour?" (Jn 12:27).

This prayer shows there was no limitation upon the Father's control of events, upon the freedom of his decisions which were never subject to blind fatality.

Even so, after Jesus had expressed his anguish, he added: "But it was for this that I came to this hour" (Jn 12:27). He was fully aware that his whole earthly life had been leading up to this supreme hour and that the coherence of his life demanded this denouement. Its inevitability stemmed not only from the Father's will but also from Jesus' deepest longing. He would bring to perfect fulfillment the love for which he had come into the world by laying down his life for his friends (cf. Jn 15:13).

Now we can understand the meaning of the hour more clearly. The Father had not simply decreed an hour, but an hour into which all the love of Christ would be concentrated, an hour that would sum up his whole life with incredible density.

Beyond that, the hour which was to be the hour of his passing "from this world to the Father" (Jn 13:1), was not only the hour of the Passion but also the hour of his glorious triumph: "The hour has come for the Son of Man to be glorified" (Jn 12:23). "Father, the hour has come! Give glory to your Son that your Son may give glory to you, inasmuch as you have given him authority over all mankind, that he may bestow eternal life on those you gave him" (Jn 17:1-2).

This hour also included Jesus' passage from time to eternity. It was not merely the compression of the temporal dimension of a human life. It also signified the insertion of human time into eternal life. It was at once an hour of earthly time and an hour of eternity.

This "hour" had effects for the world of eternity as well as for the world of time, because the Son of Man gave his life for both the living and the dead. For the deceased, this was the hour of salvation, the fulfillment of the hope of all who had lived before Christ: "I solemnly assure you, an hour is coming, has indeed come, when the dead shall hear the voice of the Son of God, and

those who have heeded it shall live" (Jn 5:25; cf. 5:28).
For those who were still alive, it was the hour of a new
religion: "Yet an hour is coming, and is already here,
when authentic worshipers will worship the Father in
Spirit and in truth" (Jn 4:23). True worship was liberated from its particularistic limitations: "An hour is coming when you will worship the Father neither on this
mountain nor in Jerusalem" (Jn 4:21).

The "hour" is thus particularly rich in meaning. We
can affirm that in the whole of human history there was
never another moment like this one. It was a unique hour
that gave a new dimension to human time. Let us again
sum up its distinctive marks: The hour summed up the
whole of Jesus' life, and with it all the hopes mankind
had cherished until that time. Decreed by the Father,
it was an act of God's omnipotence affecting the temporal
unfolding of this world. As the passage from Christ's
Passion to his glorification, it signified the emergence of
time into eternity. It inaugurated a new life in eternity
for the deceased, and a new life on earth for the living
in which spiritual universalism was to supplant local
particularisms. In short, it was the decisive, plenary hour
when the limits of time and space were exceeded and
when, in consequence, hope assumed new dimensions.

Eschatological Hope

The eschatological expectation of the Old Covenant
found expression in Jesus' apocalyptic discourse. This
discourse presents us with the problem of the real significance of Christ's eschatological hope.

Was Jesus deluded in his hope? Did he hope for and
announce an imminent end for the earthly world? Several Protestant exegetes have spoken of an essential error
on Christ's part, of such proportions as to bring down

"one of the pillars of Christianity." Such was the view of D. F. Strauss.[1] Others have simply seen it as an unimportant mistake regarding the length of the prospective delay.[2] The case of G. Beasley-Murray is of special interest. He would have preferred not to attribute such an error to Jesus, but declared he was obliged to do so when confronted with the evidence of the text.[3] After a study focussing on the eschatological discourse in Mark, he concluded that it must be accepted as the authentic thinking of Jesus.[4] It might be easier to solve the problem by classifying the discourse simply as a narrative,[5] a passage put together by the Evangelist. This would eliminate Jesus' own teaching from consideration. However, we tend to agree with Beasley-Murray that the discourse is in substance a faithful rendition of Christ's words.

Let us briefly indicate how the interpretation of this text, by respecting the authenticity of the discourse, leads us to the conclusion not only that Jesus was not mistaken in his eschatological hope but that he also revealed its scope and definitive meaning.

Jesus clearly declared that the events announced for the end of the world were to occur in the immediate future: the profanation of the Temple which he called "the abominable and destructive presence" (Mk 13:14), the greatest disaster since the creation of the world, the cosmic mourning on the day of the Lord, the glorious coming of the Son of Man on a cloud and the gathering of the elect (Mk 13:14-27; Mt 24:15-31; Lk 21:20-28).

These prophetic visions were to be fulfilled without delay: "I assure you, this generation will not pass away until all these things take place. The heavens and the earth will pass away but my words will not pass" (Mk 13:30-31; Mt 24:34-35; Lk 21:32-33).

However, let us not conclude that to Jesus' mind the end of the world was imminent. The eschatological discourse makes a very clear distinction between this final outcome and the catastrophe foretold. The latter is not presented as the end, but rather as the beginning of tribulations (Mk 13:7-8; Mt 24:6-7). While Jesus insisted on the imminence of disaster, he declared he did not know the exact time of the end of the world: "As to the exact day or hour, no one knows it, neither the angels in heaven nor even the Son, but only the Father" (Mk 13:32; Mt 24:36).

Jesus did not specifically describe the imminent disaster. He merely referred to it in the prophetic images of the Old Testament. While he promised these images would be realized, we should not interpret his words to mean a literal or concrete realization. We must recognize them for what they are, namely, images. Despite their diversity, they were used to indicate one and the same reality.

This reality is essentially defined in the context of the two themes so often discerned in the eschatological discourse: the destruction of the Temple of Jerusalem and the collapse of the cosmos.

In other circumstances, Jesus used the image of the destruction of the Temple to signify his own death. In fact, his conviction by the religious authorities of the Jewish people signified the spiritual destruction of Judaism and of its sanctuary. The tearing of the Temple veil at the moment of Jesus' death, recorded by the Evangelists, symbolically confirmed it. From the time of Jesus' death, God's presence was no longer centered in the Jewish people. The abominable and destructive presence now stood "where it should not be" (Mk 13:14), and there remained not a stone upon a stone of the Temple because the whole reason for its existence had disappeared.

Luke alluded to the siege of Jerusalem by the Roman armies in connection with Jesus' prophetic words on the destruction of the Temple.[6] This contributed to the view that Jesus had announced the destruction of the year 70 A.D., whereas his prophecy was addressed to another level of reality, the spiritual and religious, in which the destruction of the Temple signified his death to be followed by his Resurrection (Jn 2:20-22).

Far more terrifying is the canvas depicting the collapse of the cosmos in total darkness: "During that period . . . the sun will be darkened, the moon will not shed its light, stars will fall out of the skies, and the heavenly hosts will be shaken" (Mk 13:24-25). Lagrange warned against too literal an acceptance of these apocalyptic descriptions that associate inanimate nature with the events of history. He also pointed out that at a later epoch the image of the darkening of the stars was used in Jewish funerary inscriptions to depict mourning for individuals.[7] The account of Jesus' death suggests to us in what sense a prophecy was fulfilled which, according to the Old Testament, was intended to describe the end of the world (cf. Is 13:9-13).

Darkness fell over the whole land from the sixth to the ninth hour (cf. Mk 15:33; Mt 27:45; Lk 23:44). To say "the whole land," and not merely the environs of Golgotha, was plunged in darkness shows this was not an observation by witnesses at the site of the event, but a doctrinal note on the cosmic repercussions of Christ's death. Here the image takes on its full significance. In attacking Jesus, the powers of darkness (cf. Lk 22:53) attacked the whole world. In this sense, we might say that the Savior's death was the end of the world.

The coming of the Son of Man on the clouds and the gathering up of the elect after the cosmic disaster do not refer to the Parousia or to what has been called the last judgment. Rather they concern the more immediate event of the coming of the glorious Christ into the world and the gathering up of all mankind into his Church. In his response to Caiphas, Jesus announced the Son of Man would come "soon" (cf. Mt 26:62-64).

Using these images to describe imminent events in the history of salvation, Jesus demythified the prophecies of the last days. He unveiled the reality hinted at by the descriptions of ultimate catastrophe and final triumph. He thereby showed that he was to fulfill the hope of the Jewish people. The time was no longer one of promise but of fulfillment.

Jesus' disciples had not understood his words. Under the prophetic and apocalyptic descriptions they held on to the old Jewish hope. Assured that its fulfillment was imminent and not realizing it had already come to pass in Jesus, they looked for a universal disaster and centered their hope on a Parousia in the near future. And yet Jesus' words, as they have been transmitted to us by the Evangelists, reveal an entirely different line of thinking. The greatest trial of human history, according to Christ's own words, would not be delayed until a distant end of the world. The central eschatological event was to be the death and glorious coming of the Son of Man. The hope Jesus wanted to communicate to his disciples was founded on an eschatological fulfillment beginning, in his words, "now."

Christ's Death and the Transition to the Third Day

For Jesus, death always involved a life beyond the grave. The object of hope, as he presented it, was in the transition from death to the triumph of life.

When Jesus announced the death of the Son of Man, he did not stop at this prediction, which in itself could only be a cause for sadness. He also announced his Resurrection (Mk 8:31; 9:31; 10:33-34). The mention of "three days" is significant. The reason he continually specified this delay was to make clear that his passage from death to the life of glory would be of very short duration. He was not speaking of the resurrection "on the last day" (cf. Jn 11:24), in some nebulous future, but of a resurrection that would just allow death time to occur in order to triumph over it.

Recently research has been undertaken on the meaning of the three days' delay. To explain how it fulfilled Scripture, efforts have been made to clarify the meaning of the passage from Hosea: "Come, let us return to the Lord, for it is he who has rent, but he will heal us; he has struck us, but he will bind our wounds. He will revive us after two days; on the third day he will raise us up, to live in his presence" (Ho 6:1-2). The reference to this text has the merit at least of suggesting that the destiny of the entire people was involved in the three days' delay.[8] Jesus' resurrection on the third day called to mind the raising up of the people of God after times of trial.

The third day may be viewed as the day the Covenant was concluded,[9] or in a more general perspective as the day of salvation.[10]

However, the theological significance of the third day should not overshadow its historical reality.[11]

The third day is not simply a figure of speech. In his predictions, Jesus mentioned it as an intrinsic element of the historical fulfillment. He wanted his hearers to understand, after the event, how clearly it had been prophesied. He thus guaranteed the fulfillment of the hope he sought to inspire.

Besides, the interval of three days was necessary for death and resurrection to be seen in their strict reality. During this interval, only a passage to immortality was possible. Now, Jesus suffered real and total death, and his Resurrection was not merely a survival. It was the authentic return of his body to life in a glorious state.

The interval stresses how both events were part of the earthly life of mankind. Whereas the Old Testament had visualized resurrection as an event to occur in an indefinite future not linked to human history, Jesus was announcing the Resurrection of the Son of Man as a present reality. This event was to occur within his own time.

There is an important implication here as to the nature of hope. This is not because the number three has any special significance in preference to any other. But specifying the day helped to show that God had decreed a delay, and the concrete circumstances of Jesus' Resurrection were already decided. Once the exact date of his death was known, the date of his return to life would be equally immune from error. Thus we are presented with a hope that cannot be disappointed because it is contained in a divine plan to be realized in human history.

Equally noteworthy is the fact that the moment of the Resurrection was determined in relation to Jesus' death. He did not reveal in advance on what day he would die, or on what day he would rise again. From the point of view of hope, what mattered was the link between the two events, their sequence in time.

Hope and the Challenge of Sin

The hope expressed by Jesus was assured of triumph over the greatest obstacle to human hope, namely, sin.

Before Jesus entered upon his Passion, he understood perfectly what it would mean. He knew it was the price to be paid for liberating mankind. He knew he was the Son of God who had come to serve and to give his life in ransom for many (cf. Mk 10:45; Mt 20:28).

More than anyone else, Jesus realized the extent of sin's ravages throughout the world. During his public life he denounced even the most hidden forms of moral evil.

In confronting the hostility of those who refused to believe in him, he experienced the force of human freedom, capable of stubbornly resisting God. We have many indications that he was deeply disturbed by this resistance. His apostrophe to Jesusalem (cf. Mt 23:27) showed this in a special way. Jesus' mission might well be called hopeless, inasmuch as it ended in the failure of death on a cross.

However, it was precisely in what appeared to be his ultimate failure, humanly speaking, in the face of the forces of sin, that Jesus saw his definitive and total victory: ". . . now will this world's prince be driven out, and I—once I am lifted up from earth—will draw all men to myself" (Jn 12:31-32).

Thus, the most heinous of sins, rejecting the Savior and putting him to death, was mysteriously integrated into God's plan. For the reign of sin among men was destroyed through Jesus' sacrifice. Where evil had seemed to triumph, hope really won the day.

This is the paradox of hope. It is not weakened by the propagation of evil, for it knows that with the manifestation of sin comes the even greater victory of God's holiness. On the eve of his Passion, Jesus said to his disciples: "the Prince of this world is at hand" (Jn 14:30). Then, when he was arrested, he declared to those who were laying hold of him: "this is your hour—the triumph of darkness!" (Lk 22:53).

Equally paradoxical is Jesus' certitude that he would draw all men to himself at the very moment he seemed rejected or abandoned by everyone. Obviously, a hope of this magnitude is not based on human reasons but on the power of God.

Moreover, this hope assumed the form of a prayer in which Jesus declared he expected from the Father not only his personal victory over sin but the triumph of his Church. His priestly prayer announced and demanded holiness of his disciples, a holiness to be achieved not outside the world but within it, in an ambience where sin was wreaking its ravages. Jesus did not hesitate to send his disciples into the world. He was not afraid to expose them to the dangers of warring against the forces of evil. He made it clear that Christian hope must not seek the security of perseverance from the vantage point of a safe refuge. He counted on the omnipotence of the Father who had consecrated his disciples in the truth (cf. Jn 17:17), communicating to them a holiness strong enough to resist all assaults and to spread his life-giving influence over the whole world.

The boldness of Christ's hope was all the more re-markable inasmuch as Satan had already won a victory within his chosen circle of disciples. During the Last Supper, Judas had determined to betray him. This defection certainly caused Jesus deep grief, but he did not let this defeat mar his optimistic vision of the future. He did not let it shrivel his hope to the point of driving him to measures of protection and apartness. "I do not ask you to take them out of the world, but to guard them from the evil one" (Jn 17:15).

In the same prayer Jesus unfolded his lofty dream of unity. He asked for perfect unity among his disciples, unity in the image of the union between him and his Father: "I pray . . . that all may be one as you, Father, are in me, and I in you; I pray that they may be [one] in us, that the world may believe that you sent me" (Jn 17:20-21). He therefore expected his disciples to give brilliant witness of this union, and thus kindle the faith of many others.

As it happened, Jesus' hope had just been challenged in this area also. At the Last Supper the disciples had revived their quarreling over the first place. It was evident that humanly speaking there was no depending on their good intentions to achieve harmony in the future.

As soon as Jesus disappeared from the scene, his disciples' rivalries would rekindle. Hope was to respond to this challenge by giving the disciples a unity that descended on them as a divine gift, a gift that Jesus had already asked for them: "I have given them the glory you gave me that they may be one, as we are one . . . that their unity may be complete" (Jn 17:22-23).

This gift stemmed from Jesus' sacrifice: "Jesus would die . . . to gather into one all the dispersed children of God" (Jn 11:52). Because of Christ's death, Christian hope is certain it can overcome all the divisions in which mankind reveals its sinfulness.

Hope and the Challenge of Suffering

Jesus proclaimed two certitudes on the subject of death. The first concerns immortality: "The man who loves his life loses it, while the man who hates his life in this world preserves it to life eternal" (Jn 12:25; cf. Mk 8:34; Lk 9:24). Death is not a loss but a gain, a passage to eternal life, in the measure that it comes about through a gift of self.

The second certitude is even more consoling. It concerns the fruitfulness of sacrifice: "I solemnly assure you, unless the grain of wheat falls to the earth and dies, it remains just a grain of wheat. But if it dies, it produces much fruit" (Jn 12:24). The image of the grain of wheat does not explain the why's and wherefores of this fruitfulness, but at least it has the advantage of stressing death's grandeur. Death, instead of being the extinction of a life, dooming it to ultimate sterility, is the wellspring of a superabundant vitality that enriches others.

Equally illuminating is Jesus' comparison of death with the pains of childbirth: "When a woman is in labor she is sad that her time has come. When she has borne her child, she no longer remembers her pain for joy that a man has been born into the world" (Jn 16:21). Jesus used this image to announce the transition from sadness to joy that was to characterize the disciples' participation in his Passion: "In the same way, you are sad for a time, but I shall see you again; then your hearts will rejoice with a joy no one can take from you" (Jn 16:22). Still, we must not forget that the roots of joy lie in the fruitfulness of tribulation and that joy is the result of a new life. Through the Passion a new man came into being.

No other figure of speech could have expressed so well the meaning of the hope bound up with suffering. We have already noted that sufferings of all kinds that weigh heavily on the human condition are a powerful challenge to hope. The challenge is met by the conviction that suffering does not condemn a person to a diminished life, but instead brings forth a new life, for himself and for others as well.

This conviction shines through a number of Jesus' other recorded statements: "Just as Moses lifted up the serpent in the desert, so must the Son of Man be lifted up, that all who believe may have eternal life in him" (Jn 3:14-15). "Yet I tell you the sober truth: It is much better for you that I go. If I fail to go, the Paraclete will never come to you, whereas if I go, I will send him to you" (Jn 16:7).

Also predicated on death is the pouring out of the Holy Spirit who since Pentecost has been the fountainhead of the developing Church as well as of each individual Christian life.

Such a perspective places us far above the conception of suffering that imbued the Old Testament: the conception of a suffering sent by God as a punishment for sinners. Jesus himself expressly excluded such an interpretation of suffering when he affirmed that the man born blind owed his infirmity neither to his own sins nor to those of his parents (Jn 9:3), and that the victims of massacres or disasters were no more guilty than others (Lk 13:2). Above all, his Passion demonstrated the positive and life-giving value of suffering.

Instead of confining the Christian's horizons to a sinful past, suffering invites him to look to a better future. Instead of looking backward, it turns in the opposite direction, that of hope. As a result, trials become less burdensome, for there is no greater torment than to think of oneself as doomed to make atonement for the past. Christ brought suffering and death back into the stream of life, giving them a power of regeneration.

Admittedly, we still need to discover for ourselves through faith and hope the meaning of the trials and tribulations of life. But in principle no misfortune in the course of human history is unrelated to the death of Christ. For his death, the greatest disaster that ever happened since the creation of the world, carried within it all the hope of a new humanity. Sufferings accepted in this spirit are truly bearers of life.

We should pay special note to the words Jesus uses in John's text to describe his Passion and death: "and I—once I am lifted up from earth—" (Jn 12:32). He was referring to his death on the cross. In addition, his words have a symbolic meaning. They call to mind the glorious raising up of the suffering servant, promised long before (Is 52:13). This allows us to see an intimate bond between suffering and the glorification of Christ, applicable to all pain united to the pain of the Redemption. For the Christian, to suffer is "to be lifted up," to ascend morally and spiritually. This is not to imply that in suffering we want to "lift ourselves up" by our own efforts in order to gain greater mastery over our personality after the manner of the Stoics who claimed they could dominate their pain through serene indifference.

We are "lifted up," elevated by God to a superior level of life and fruitfulness. Through suffering we can become more receptive to the divine gift that transforms man. The answer to the challenge of suffering is given by the Father himself. Man receives the power to exceed himself, and share in the love by which the Father gave his Son as a sacrifice for the salvation and the uplifting of the human community.

The Personal Trial of Hope

Even though Jesus was absolutely sure of the fruitfulness of suffering and death, his hope was put to the test.

According to John's Gospel, after Jesus had affirmed that when the grain of wheat dies it bears much fruit and the person who renounces his life obtains life eternal, he was filled with deep anxiety: "My soul is troubled now" (Jn 12:27). And so we must not think that hope, however firm and fervent, can succeed in eliminating all fear and revulsion in the face of suffering. Yet hope can overcome them, as was the case with Jesus who embraced the divine plan and asked that it be fulfilled: "But it was for this that I came to this hour. Father, glorify your name!" Then a heavenly voice responded: "I have glorified it, and will glorify it again" (Jn 12:27-29).

The anguish Jesus experienced was the surfacing of a sentiment already hidden within him. During his public life, in unspecified circumstances, he had said: "I have a baptism to receive. What anguish I feel till it is over!" (Lk 12:50).

The foreboding of this baptism wrenched Jesus' heart to the point that some have called it "a permanent Gethsemani."[12] Such a description is too violent. Jesus continually visualized the death he was destined to suffer.

Throughout his life, Jesus had to fight off the instinctive revulsion any man would feel at the prospect of such a tragic destiny. The word "baptism" suggests that the trial endured would culminate in a new birth. It thus implies a hope, but a hope that must pass through the crucible of suffering.

We have a sign that Gethsemani proved to be a trial of hope in Mark's comment: "Then he began to be filled with fear and distress" (Mk 14:33). It was not a distress amounting to a strong revulsion, but rather an overpowering weariness, a moment of depression when nothing seemed to make sense, a lassitude that impelled to flight.[13]

Such sentiments would tend to extinguish hope in most other men. Jesus experienced them firsthand. He chose to share the emotions of all who ever have been or ever will be weary with life, with themselves, and with the world. Those who have lost their zest for living, those who "can't take any more," can turn to the Christ of Gethsemani as someone who can understand them because he has passed through the same kind of a crisis.

How did Jesus fight to keep up his hope during this hour of darkness? His fellowship with the Father, renewed with greater intensity in prayer, kept him firm despite his interior struggle. According to Luke, as in the case of the distress recorded by John, consolation came to him from heaven in response to his prayer. Hope can subsist only as a divine gift continuously sought and received.

The first words Jesus spoke from the cross expressed heroic love for his enemies, and also rang out like a cry of hope: "Father, forgive them; they do not know what they are doing" (Lk 23:34). This request for his enemies' forgiveness indicates that Jesus hoped for the conversion of those who had condemned him to death. Although he was the victim of malicious intrigues, he did not consider his enemies to be irremediably lost. And yet their obstinacy in heaping insults on the crucified should have made clear that theirs was a desperate case. Even their taunts were addressed to Jesus' hope: "Save yourself . . ." (Mk 15:30; Mt 27:40). Though his hope was sorely tested, it bounced back in an effort to save his most intransigent enemies. He refused to admit any limits to his hope for the salvation of men.

Here we see a victory won by hope in the specific context of persecution that lighted the way the disciples were to follow. Charity must overcome the hostility of persecutors, and to this end it needs to be sustained by hope. Hope in turn attains lofty heights when, in the face of rancor or cruelty, violence or ridicule, it continues to anticipate the moral transformation of enemies.

On the cross, Jesus' hope was probed to even greater depths, as indicated by his cry of dereliction: "My God, my God, why have you forsaken me?" (Mk 15:34; Mt 27:46). What really thwarts hope is the sense of being abandoned from on high, of being cut off from the divine covenant, of being the victim of God's absence. Jesus knew that the Father remained with him, as he had already declared (cf. Jn 16:32). But he no longer had the affective sense of his Father's presence. In this spiritual vacuum, he again had recourse to prayer: "Father, into your hands I commend my spirit" (Lk 23:46). This act of abandonment was filled with hope. In commending his spirit to the Father, Jesus was expecting a new spiritual life from him. This time heaven's response would be the event of the Resurrection.

The test of Jesus' hope was the prototype of the trials his disciples were to suffer after him. It is the destiny of Christian hope to be under constant attack, to face deep inner struggles, anguish, weariness, lassitude, and at times to be overwhelmed by persecution and the sense of God's absence. Amid these trials, the Christian is invited to transform his hope into a prayer that expects all things from the Father's hands.

NOTES FOR CHAPTER FOUR

1. **Vie de Jésus,** (French translation by Littré), Paris, 1864, p. 339.
2. O. Cullman, **Christ et le temps,** Neuchâtel, 1947, p. 106.
3. **Jesus and the Future,** London, 1954, p. 183.
4. **A Commentary on Mark Thirteen,** New York, 1957.
5. Cf. for this view J. Lambrecht, **Die Redaktion der Markus—Apokalypse, Literarische Analyse und Strukturuntersuchung,** Rome, 1967.
6. Cf. Lk. 21:20-24. Compare this passage with the much more mysterious text of Mark, (13:14), and Matthew, (24:15): "When you see the abominable and destructive thing . . . standing on holy ground. . . ." Luke, writing after the year 70 A.D., reinterpreted the text according to the event he believed Jesus had foretold.
7. **Le Messianisme chez les juifs,** Paris, 1909, pp. 47-49.
8. The allusion is not invalidated by the fact that the text of Hosea was not Messianic. Cf. J. Dupont, **Etudes sur les Actes des Apôtres,** Paris, 1967, p. 332.
9. This is J. Wijngaards' interpretation in, **Death and Resurrection in Covenant Context,** (Hos. 6:1-2), **Vetus Testamentum** 17, 1967), pp. 226-239, who explains the third day in the context of covenant, the pact usually being celebrated on the morning of the third day.
10. This has been shown by K. Lehmann, **Auferweckt am dritten Tag nach der Sshrift,** Freiburg, 1968, based on the Targums and the Midrashim.
11. On this point, we disagree with the position adopted by Lehmann as being exegetically unjustifiable.
12. M. J. Lagrange, **Evangile selon S. Luc,** Paris, 1927, p. 273, which makes use of Plummer's expression.
13. V. Taylor stresses that the use of the verb "he began" expresses a very powerful and deep emotion, and refers to Swete's remark on the subject of **adèmonein:** "distress following upon a great shock," (**The Gospel according to St. Mark,** London, 1966, p. 552).

CHAPTER V

RESURRECTION AND HOPE

A New Hope is Born

Within its historical context, Jesus' Resurrection appears not as the fruit of his disciples' hope but rather as the wellspring of their hope.

It is certainly true that the Resurrection is one of the fruits of Christ's hope. His whole life, including his final offering in death, had been directed toward the Resurrection. We have seen that Jesus' hope of a glorious triumph ascended to the Father in the form of a prayer, and the Resurrection was the Father's answer to his prayer. Such is the thinking of the author of **Hebrews** when he speaks of the one who "in the days when he was in the flesh . . . offered prayers and supplications with loud cries and tears to God" and who "was heard because of his reverence" (Heb 5:7).[1] The Father who possesses all life liberated Jesus from death by answering the prayer of his sacrifice and giving him the new life of the Resurrection.

This reveals the importance of hope insofar as it involves human cooperation in the fulfillment of God's plan. God first makes us hope for the gifts he intends to give us. When we hope all our aspirations are involved, and thus God is not alone in wanting the awaited event. Rather, the event results from the joining of the human will to God's.

So Jesus had to ask and hope for his Resurrection.

While the event was part of God's pre-ordained plan, it was foreseen by him as his response to human hope, and in particular to the hope of Jesus. The entire future of mankind began to take shape in this hope.

On the contrary, the hope of the disciples had not kept pace with their Master's. We have spoken of the crisis Jesus' death had caused among them. They were filled with suspicions and doubts not only in the face of the news the women brought them, but even in the presence of Christ himself after he returned into their midst. Their suspicions and doubts were confirmed by the earliest tradition. If it had not been so, no one would have dared to attribute such attitudes to the men whom the Christian community looked upon as witnesses of the Resurrection.

It might be said that the disciples became witnesses of the Resurrection in spite of themselves. The reason they were so hard to convince was that their hope had died with Jesus. It was only when they were forced to acknowledge that their Master had truly risen that their hope was reborn.

It would be an error to think that the crumbling of the disciples' hope at Calvary was purely a human accident. In God's plans this failure was destined to reveal more clearly the newness of Christian hope. This hope is fundamentally different from that of the Jews because it rests on the event of the Resurrection.

Just as Jesus' death signalled the end of Judaism with the tearing of the Temple veil, it also meant the end of a hope limited to the Jewish people and to their national aspirations. It even meant the end of the prophetic hope that had not risen to an expectation of the Incarnation or of the Messiah's Resurrection. The advent of a new religion and of new relations between God and men was the birth of a new hope. Like the Temple, hope was destroyed, to be rebuilt in three days.

Christian hope, therefore, has its own unique character. It was historically determined by Christ's Resurrection, and that is why it stands apart from every other hope.

The Temporal Dimension of Resurrection and Hope

When the risen Jesus appeared to his disciples, he told them: "Look at my hands and my feet; it is really I" (Lk 24:39). He chose to be recognized in his physical identity. This body was indeed the one that had suffered on the cross and still bore the marks of the crucifixion. He allowed Thomas to confirm this identity by placing his finger in the marks of the nails and his hand in the opening in his side (cf. Jn 20:27).[2]

The fact that Jesus presented himself in his corporeal reality does not mean that his Resurrection was a return to the physical life of his mortal years. From this point of view, Jesus' Resurrection differed essentially from the resurrections he himself had brought to others. The daughter of Jairus, the son of the widow of Naim, and Lazarus had simply resumed their earthly lives without undergoing any transformations by reason of their passage through death.

In Jesus' case, it is evident he did not resume his mortal life. He appeared in his risen body only a few times, and then in a mysterious manner that demonstrated he could move about freely at will. In fact, his sudden apparitions made witnesses wonder if it were really he and not a ghost. He attested that he now possessed a life of a superior sort, endowed with bodily properties that exceeded those of physical matter. It was because this new condition differed so radically from his mortal state that he offered to let his disconcerted disciples verify his identity for themselves.

Now, in affirming his identity, Jesus confirmed the
"I am" or the "it is I" that he had announced earlier,
especially during his trial when he had expressed the
conviction he would live after his execution.

It was by his Resurrection that Jesus demonstrated
his immutability. When he said "It is I," he did not
merely seek recognition as a lost friend who had been
found again. He let it be understood that the divine identity he had claimed with veiled words was more clearly
discernible in his resurrected body.

This means that from the moment of his Resurrection
divine eternity permeated Jesus' body, raising it up to
a superior level of life. The Resurrection involved a
certain divinization. It was the welling up of divine life
in the humanity of Jesus.

From this point of view, the Resurrection completed
the mystery of the Incarnation. The latter had been a
transition from time to eternity. The flesh of the Word
which, during Jesus' earthly life, had simply shared the
ordinary condition of other mortals, now acceded to a
glorious, spiritualized and divinized life. The Incarnation
reached its limit when the divine penetrated and transformed all that was human in Christ.

Keeping these things in mind, we can now define the
temporal dimension of the Resurrection as a state beyond
time yet existing in time. Whence the difficulty of situat-
ing Christ's Resurrection within the context of history.
There has been debate whether the Resurrection should
be classified as an historical event. It obviously has a
metahistorical aspect in that it involved the passage of
Jesus' body to eternal life. Because of this, it is not verifiable in its specific nature as resurrection. All that anyone could ascertain about the event at the time was the
fact that the corpse had disappeared. The only introduction the women and disciples had to the mystery of the
Resurrection was the discovery of an empty tomb. The

passage to eternal life cannot be the object of empirical observation, because it involves a rupture with time.

However, from another point of view the Resurrection is truly an historical event because it occurred at a specific moment in the history of mankind. We have already stressed the historical significance of the date of the third day. It was on the third day after Jesus' death that his body was filled with a divine life that made it spring forth from the tomb.

In addition, the apparitions of the risen Christ were proof of his intention to remain present to mankind and to history. After his Resurrection Jesus was in some way detached from the sequence of time, since he would appear unexpectedly, letting others see him, then disappear without regard for the laws of temporal succession. And yet he affirmed his presence and his nearness to the temporal life of his disciples. The Resurrection did not snatch Jesus from human time. On the contrary, it allowed him to enter human time with far greater freedom.

Since Christian hope is founded on the Resurrection, it, too, takes on a temporal dimension that involves the presence of eternity within time. That is why it cannot be described as simply relating the present to the future within time and eternity. It exists in a time that has in a certain sense become eternal and divine.

By this very fact Christian hope is profoundly different from other hopes that spring up among men, and simply anticipate fulfillment within a given span of time. Christian hope is rooted in eternal life, which, through Christ's Resurrection, has transformed the temporal condition of mankind.

To return to a Biblical symbol, the third day inaugurated a new mode of temporal succession. Coming after the first day of creation when the world came forth into the light and after the day of trial when it was plunged in darkness, the day of the Resurrection raised the universe to new heights in which time was immersed in eternity.

A Lasting Fellowship

How does the eternization of time, implicit in the mystery of the Resurrection, enter into human existence?

Let us seek the answer in some of Jesus' own words. First of all, let us call to mind the certitude that hovers over the development of the Church and of each Christian life: "And know that I am with you always, until the end of the world!" (Mt 28:20).

This promise is remarkable in its vision of the future that situates the life of the disciples in the context of the final completion of the world, of a "consummation" which their mission will help to bring about. The horizons of the Christian life embrace the universe in its spatial and temporal totality, as well as its ultimate perfection.

There is something even more powerful about the promise. It is the "I am with you always" that sustains hope not merely with a vision of future triumph and historical completion, but by a covenant rooted in being.[3]

The "I am" is that of the risen Christ, whose entire human nature has been transformed so that he now lives a divinely eternal life. As a result, he can be with his disciples in a complete solidarity that is at once divine and human. When we compare this assurance with the one given to Moses: "I shall be with you," we realize that Jesus' promise goes much farther. God was with Moses, but still apart from him, maintaining the full distance between God and man. Jesus is with his disciples, having established a human communion with them that enables his divine being to penetrate their lives. The whole meaning of the words "to be with" rests in Christ's intended communication of himself. He shares with his disciples the power that has been given to him in heaven and on earth; he asks them to transmit his teaching (Mt 28:18-20). Above all, he wants the communication of his being to be the foundation of this mission.

If we reflect on the implications of the promise, we discover that it is precisely the communication of the divine being of the risen Christ that will enable the disciples to cover the temporal distance that separates them from the end of the world. Christ's "I am" has already covered the span of time to the end, and enables the disciples to do so with him.

This perspective helps us to better grasp the nature of hope. While it looks eagerly, unswervingly to the future, it is no less rooted in a present which, because it is joined to eternity, makes possible the attainment of this future.

The words spoken at the Last Supper point even more insistently to a presence of Christ that will remain perpetually: "Live on in me, as I do in you" (Jn 15:4).[4]

When Jesus spoke these words he was still living his earthly life, but looking forward to the time after his death. He was referring to the relationship he would have with his disciples after the Resurrection. In instituting the Eucharist, he was anticipating this Resurrection, for only in his glorious state could he give his flesh to eat and his blood to drink.

When he compared himself to the vine to which the branches must remain attached, he was referring to this same glorious state. For it is by virtue of his resurrected state that he is the source of life. As this source, he asked his disciples to live in him as he lives in them.

The term "live," when applied to interpersonal relations, may simply mean familiarity. Thus, after the first two disciples had asked Jesus where he lived, they "stayed with him that day" (Jn 1:39). In Christ's case, the word takes on a more absolute meaning when it concerns the relationship between the Father and the Son. In contrast to the slave or servant, the son lives forever in his father's house (cf. Jn 8:35). And conversely the Father lives in him, "accomplishing his works" (Jn 14:10). He is in the Father and the Father is in him.

It was in the image of his relations of mutual immanence with the Father that Jesus wanted to establish his relations with his disciples. He wanted them to live in him and he in them, as he lives in the Father and the Father in him. To those who love him and keep his word, he will come, and together he and the Father will make their dwelling place with them (cf. Jn 14:23).

What Jesus wanted to assure was a share in God's own fellowship. He wanted it to be perpetual, and to have the eternal aspect this fellowship implies. His use of the preposition "in" indicates he meant this fellowship to be a communication of being. Even during their earthly lives, his disciples were called to live **in him,** as he lived **in them.**

Evidently, such a sharing in the divine fellowship depends on human consent, freely given. The disciples remained responsible for their actions, and it was only by obeying Jesus' commands that they could live in him and have him live in them. But if they conformed to the Master's will, their mutual indwelling with him would take on its full power and they would share in the eternity of divine being.

Through this mutual indwelling hope escapes the evanescence of time. Amid the blows that might threaten to destroy it, hope preserves an essential stability that comes to it from the stability of God himself, shared in and through the risen Christ.

The Passage From Death to The Resurrection

Although hope lives by Christ's Resurrection, it knows that Christian living involves a participation in the Savior's Passion and death. Paul expressed this truth in compelling terms: "I have been crucified with Christ" (Gal 2:19).

In Paul's eyes, the time that measures out human life is determined by the accomplishment of the Passion in the individual Christian's life: "Even now I find my joy in the suffering I endure for you. In my own flesh I fill up what is lacking in the sufferings of Christ for the sake of his body, the church" (Col 1:24). He did not claim he filled up in his flesh what might have been missing to Christ's Passion considered in itself. For nothing was lacking to the sufferings Christ endured during the drama of his Passion. They sufficed to obtain the total reconciliation of mankind with God, the remission of all sins, and the granting of salvation. Paul never doubted the all-encompassing value of Jesus' "blood." In this passage, Paul was not speaking of Christ's trials in themselves, but of these trials as experienced in his flesh, that is to say, by his participation in the Passion. He had to personally live Christ's sufferings, and this participation was not yet ended. Something was lacking, for at the time Paul wrote the Letter to the Colossians he was in prison and had not yet finished his own slow martyrdom.[5]

Hope cannot deny this fundamental necessity. It must go even further, and embrace it. This means that Christian hope must be lived as an unceasing passage from death to resurrection. Paul admirably explained it in referring to the trials of his apostolic ministry: "Continually we carry about in our bodies the dying of Jesus, so that in our bodies the life of Jesus may also be revealed. While we live we are constantly being delivered to death for Jesus' sake, so that the life of Jesus may be revealed in our mortal flesh. Death is at work in us, but life in you" (2 Cor 4:10-12).

Far from discouraging hope, conformity with the Passion of Christ constantly impels hope onward and upward, because Christ's Passion is a passage to the new life of the Resurrection. That is why Paul could write: "We are afflicted in every way possible, but we are not crushed; full of doubts, we never despair. We are persecuted but never abandoned; we are struck down but never destroyed" (2 Cor 4:8-9). This might well be called a hymn to hope, even though the word "hope" is not used. Amid his trials, a Christian always quivers with hope because the death of Christ as lived in the apostle inevitably culminates in a superior life.

Therefore, suffering is never the end of everything. The risen Christ clearly explained this to the disciples of Emmaus, to restore their lost hope: "Did not the Messiah have to undergo all this so as to enter into his glory?" (Lk 24:26). He wanted to show those who were disheartened by the disaster of Calvary that this disaster was the harbinger of triumph. So, too, every participation in the Passion is the sign of a deeper penetration into the mystery of the Resurrection.

This conviction likewise extends to the notion of fruitfulness. According to Paul, the passage from death to life is not for the sake of the apostle only, but for those to whom he addresses his apostolic efforts. Suffering produces fruits of life in others.[6] Paul was convinced that Christ's bodily sufferings contributed to the development of the Church. By reason of this fact, hope acquires a perspective that goes far beyond the individual, a perspective that conforms to the mystery of the Resurrection. For not only was the Resurrection the triumph of the divine life in Jesus, it was also the great event of salvation for all mankind.

There remains another important point to make regarding Jesus' passage from death to the Resurrection, that must constantly be relived by Christian hope. It is that Christ has already risen and the Christian can unite himself to his Passion only by living still more completely by his Resurrection. This may seem paradoxical, but it is nonetheless true. The passage from death to the Resurrection is accomplished in the person after he has been grasped by the risen Christ. The Resurrection enables the individual Christian to overcome his trials by its very presence in his life.

After saying he is "crucified with Christ," Paul adds: "the life I live now is not my own; Christ is living in me" (Gal 2:20). Now, the Christ who lived in Paul was the glorious Christ. It was Christ who made Paul relive the crucifixion. And so we see that the mystery of the Passion can be lived only within the mystery of the Resurrection. This is the fundamental law of hope.

A result of this law is that when suffering comes to him the Christian is already in a certain sense beyond it. Just as we have spoken of a duration beyond time within time, we must also speak of a state beyond suffering within suffering. This is why Paul could say: "Even now I find joy in the suffering I endure for you" (Col 1:24). Here lies the justification of the beatitudes proclaimed by Jesus for all who would be associated to his sacrifice by poverty, tears, or persecution. The happiness of the glorious triumph is already present within the trial experienced. Hope contains a joy that exceeds trials at the very moment they are most overwhelming.

Thus, the mystery of the Resurrection dominates the Christian's union to redemptive suffering not only as its term but also as its source and present support. The Resurrection assures the permanence and the incessant renewal of hope, as well as its increase amid sufferings.

Eternal Life

When Christ rose from the dead, mankind passed from spiritual death, incurred by sin, to a new life. Paul calls this to mind in his Letter to the Ephesians: "But God is rich in mercy; because of his great love for us he brought us to life with Christ when we were dead in sin. By this favor you were saved. Both with and in Christ he raised us up and gave us a place in the heavens" (Ep 2:4-6).

This text shows how the mystery of Christ's Resurrection and Ascension has already been accomplished in our own past and present, and finds expression in our lives here and now. We have already come into possession of the essentials for which we hope.

The new life, received through Christ's glorious triumph, is granted in a special way to the individual Christian in baptism, which Paul thinks of as a passage from death to resurrection. Speaking to the Romans, he asked: "Are you not aware that we who were baptized into Christ Jesus were baptized into his death? Through baptism into his death we were buried with him, so that, just as Christ was raised from the dead by the glory of the Father, we too might live a new life" (Rm 6:3-4).[7] He then goes on to explain at greater length how this new life is a communion with the life of "Christ, once raised from the dead," who "will never die again" (Rm 6:9).

John prefers to call this new life "eternal life." The expression "new life" places the emphasis on the difference between Christian life and life under Judaism, and shows to what degree the Jewish promise has been fulfilled and exceeded in the new covenant. The expression "eternal life" draws our attention to the presence of eternity in this life, thereby guaranteeing the fulfillment of the promises it holds for the future. It thus becomes apparent that Christian hope is of a superior kind.

The gift of eternal life is the fruit of the elevation of the Son of Man, of the Father's gift of his only Son for love of the world (Jn 3:14-16). This is the gift the good shepherd gives the sheep that listen to his voice (Jn 10: 28). Perhaps, too, it is the gift that stems from the supreme glorification of the Son by the Father (Jn 17:2).

Paul also speaks of "eternal life," but he considers it as a future life, whereas John considers it as a gift already received. Not only is the person who believes in the Son of Man destined to enjoy eternal life; he already possesses it now (Jn 3:15, 16, 36; 6:40, 47). Likewise, whoever, when he listens to the Son's word, believes in the one who sent him (Jn 5:24) also possesses eternal life. The Eucharistic meal has the same effect: "Let me solemnly assure you, if you do not eat the flesh of the Son of Man and drink his blood, you have no life in you. He who feeds on my flesh and drinks my blood has life eternal, and I will raise him up on the last day" (Jn 6:53-54).

This possession of eternal life is linked to the mutual indwelling that results from the same sacramental act: "The man who feeds on my flesh and drinks my blood remains in me and I in him" (Jn 6:56). "To remain," we have already noted, ultimately rests on the eternal permanence of divine being.

These two affirmations are closely linked, and yet not identical. The one in Jn 6:56 referring to the man who "remains in me and I in him" concerns Christ's personal relationship to his disciple that shares in the divine fellowship between the Son and the Father. The other, in Jn 6:53-54, relating to eternal life, is more directly concerned with the change in a human life, the new dimension of life conferred to man's nature. In both cases, we see divine eternity taking possession of human time, thus giving hope a superior quality or dimension.

Let us turn our attention once more to the bond between eternal life and the resurrection on the last day. This resurrection is assured not only by the already accomplished fact of Christ's Resurrection, but also by the eternal life that the mystery of this Resurrection implants in Christians. Our hope of bodily resurrection is thus based on a spiritual life here and now that guarantees the survival of the soul and calls for the final return to life of the human body.

NOTES FOR CHAPTER FIVE

1. Some exegetes have interpreted the words "he was heard" to mean that in answer to his prayer he was saved from fear. Then there would be greater emphasis on hope. But this does not seem the more probable interpretation, because Jesus asked to be saved from death and not from fear. Cf. C. Spicq, L'épître aux Hébreux, II, Paris, 1953, p. 115.

2. It appears Thomas did not accept Jesus' invitation to probe his wounds, though he could have done so. John evidently thought the body of the resurrection, while it could pass through closed doors, could also be touched. In his view, it was physically real (Cf. Barrett, St. John, p. 476).

3. It is not enough to say, as does P. Bonnard, that we must understand these words in the light of the Old Testament (Ex 3:12; Jos. 1:5, 9; Is. 41: 10; 43:5, etc.), "as the promise of a constant and infallible help granted to Christ's envoys in the world," (L'Evangile selon Saint Matthieu, Neuchâtel, 1963, p. 419). We cannot abstract the new context in which the promise is made, a context that is absolutely unheard-of in the Old Testament, because it is the glorious Christ speaking.

4. Barrett remarks that there are three possible translations (cf. St. John, pp. 395, ff.): (1) a comparison—live in me, as I live in you; (2) a condition—if you live in me, I shall live in you; (3) a mutual involvement—so that there be a reciprocal indwelling.

Barrett bases his choice of the third interpretation on Verse 5. However, the sense of the first two interpretations should, it seems, be included in the third. The model is Christ who lives in his disciples. The condition necessary for him to live in them is that they obey his commandments and remain united to him.

5. As C. F. D. Moule has rightly pointed out (The Epistles of Paul the Apostle to the Colossians and to Philemon, Cambridge, 1957, p. 76), we do not have to choose between the view that what is lacking is the individual Christian's participation in the sufferings of Christ, and the view that envisions the Church and all it must endure until the end. According to this latter opinion, the more the apostle suffers, the more he contributes to the coming of the Parousia.

6. Cf. E. B. Allo, Seconde épître aux Corinthiens, Paris, 1937, p. 115: "... death fashions the actors—refining and for that matter continually increasing their conformity to Christ and their power as spiritual intermediaries. Meanwhile life, the life of Christ that they are imitating, both in its painful aspects and in its aspects of power, is diffused ever more strongly and intensely among their spectators." The terms "actors" and "spectators" are not the most appropriate. But what matters is the idea of reproducing the death and life of Christ and its far-reaching influence.

7. As O. Kuss notes, (Der Römerbrief, I, Regensburg, 1957, p. 298), the "new life" refers to eschatological salvation already granted.

CHAPTER VI

HOPE AND THE PRESENCE OF THE HOLY SPIRIT

Hope and Fulfillment

The Christian already possesses what he hopes for. His hope stems from the permanent presence of the risen Christ in his disciples, which calls them to remain permanently in him.

On this point we definitely part company with Moltmann's theology of hope. In his view, an eschatology based on the presence of eternity would be a falsification of the Christian doctrine of hope through Greek influences.[1] We see no need to set a Greek eschatology of fulfillment in opposition to a Jewish eschatology of promise. For Christianity is the fulfillment of the promise, and Christ's Resurrection has brought eternity into the present moment of human history. Christian life implies possession of Christ. According to Paul, it is living "in Christ"; according to John, "remaining" in him.

Thus, hope cannot be described by the image of two hands held out, two empty hands containing nothing of what they desire to obtain.

Let us take as an example the hope of the life beyond expressed in the Letter to the Philippians. Paul, probably sensing the approach of death, confides to his friends of Philippi the hope that fills his soul: "I long to be freed from this life and to be with Christ" (Ph 1:23). To his mind, "to be with Christ" is the supreme happiness that awaits him after death. This is truly an admirable definition of the eternal beatitude of heaven.[2] And yet, if we wanted to give a definition of Paul's earthly life, could we not use the very same words: "to be with Christ"?

All of Paul's aspirations were directed toward a goal already attained in the darkness of life on earth. It was precisely because he was always with Christ in the darkness of faith that he yearned so intensely to be with him in the bright daylight of the vision. At the very moment Paul was writing down this wish, he already possessed the reality for which he hoped, but a hidden reality that at certain moments seemed to escape conscious sentiment, a reality still to be revealed in all its splendor.

Jesus has given us an example of this hope, a hope that already possesses what it anticipates. For while his whole life was oriented toward the Father, he already possessed the One for whom he aspired. There is no contradiction between the two affirmations: "I go to the Father" (Jn 14:12) and "I am in the Father and the Father is in me" (Jn 14:11). Present fellowship with the Father increased Jesus' human desire to possess him totally, free from the limitations of earthly life.

The same holds true of the Christian's fellowship with Christ. The Christian goes forward to meet Christ. His whole being is polarized toward this encounter as the supreme happiness. But to advance toward Christ is not to be going toward an absent person. Christ lives in the one who hungers and thirsts for him, and this beginning of fulfillment intensifies the desire to possess him in the ultimate fellowship of heaven.

Here we find the answer to an objection raised against hope, namely, that it consists in pursuing future happiness while taking no interest in this present life and foregoing the joys this earth can offer here and now. This accusation of utopianism seems to imply that to hope is to sacrifice immediately accessible benefits for some illusory goal. Why not live fully in the present, instead of seeking to live for an uncertain future?

It is not enough to answer that hope itself constitutes happiness in the present, because acceptance of life makes it good. In other words, when we live in expectation we can accept present realities, however painful.[3] For if all happiness is relegated to the future, to a distant future, it cannot dominate the present situation and inspire man's present attitudes. Beyond any doubt, present happiness can certainly be nurtured by anticipation of a happy future, but it must spring from what man is now.

The Christian cannot be content to know his hope is certain of ultimate fulfillment, and he is advancing toward a happiness that will completely satisfy his aspirations. He must be convinced that the ultimate reality is already mysteriously present within him, and that in consequence the happiness of his present life is a preparation for the happiness of heaven. The most immediately accessible happiness is the joy of living in Christ, of remaining in him, and there is no other way to live fully in the present. Union with Christ begins to satisfy the heart's yearnings here on earth. It brings a joy that cannot be snatched away even by sufferings, a joy, as Paul tells us, that increases through trials.

Christian hope, therefore, does not live solely for the future. It lives within a present that contains the seeds of this future. It actually enjoys the happiness of possessing here and now in very truth, although in a veiled and inchoate way, the goal toward which it is moving.[4]

The Present and the Future

Does the present state of hope take anything away from its reaching out to the future?

Moltmann vigorously opposes any mysticism of immediate access to God within the present as lived. He asks: if man already possesses God, what becomes of Christ's mediation and the historical reconciliation between God and man? Hope would leave no room for history, and there would no longer be a "God of hope." For, says Moltmann, the God of Exodus and of the Resurrection is not an eternal present. He promises his presence for the future. The essential mark of the God of the promise is to be a God of the future. His name is an itinerary that opens new horizons to history. Instead of being a God who is, he is a God who will be, and who calls into being what did not yet exist (cf. Rm 4:17).[5]

This opinion must be understood in the context of the doctrine it would contradict: the perspective of a transcendent existentialism which abstracts the Biblical residue of history and retains only God's present call to man. In this perspective the whole Revelation would amount to a word that God speaks to me in the present moment. The temporal dimension of salvation would thus be wiped out, together with the whole course of history and its orientation toward the future.

Moltmann is right in rejecting this misconception of time and history, and in offering an interpretation that still sees God as the God of faith, but even more as the God of hope. He rediscovers the value of the future.

However, in his reaction he goes too far. For he refutes a mysticism that would absorb the future into the present with an historical conception of the relations between God and man that absorbs the present into the future. Deeply aware of what is lacking in a theological vision restricted to the present moment, he focuses his attention on future historical development, to the point of disregarding all that this future owes to the present.[6]

The mysticism of immediate access to God does not render the reconciliation achieved in Christ useless. Indeed, it is the fruit of this reconciliation. Through Christ the Redeemer, men have access to the Father (Ep 2:18). And this access is not to be delayed to some future time. It means acceptance into his fellowship here and now: "You are . . . members of the household of God" (Ep 2:19).

The God of Exodus was the God of the promise, but the God of the Resurrection is more than that. To the extent that he is still the God of the promise, this promise is the Holy Spirit and the realization began with Pentecost. To the extent that he is a God of the future, it is because he is the God of a present from which the future will spring. The risen Christ is the divine "I am" that has taken possession of human time by permeating it with eternity. The God of the Resurrection is still a God who will be, but he is also a God who is and who has made his eternal Being totally incarnate in the historical present.

In contrast to a vision of salvation that is too exclusively futuristic, the "now" of the New Testament is more than a passage toward the future. The central point of history is not the Parousia, but the presence here and now of the glorious Christ, a presence that will finally be consummated in the Parousia. Eternity has already erupted into time, just as time has been absorbed into divine eternity, at least in the risen Christ who is the fountainhead of a new humanity. Time, therefore, is no longer merely a succession of instants whose value lies wholly in what is to come. The newness to unfold in the future stems from the newness that has already come into being: ". . . if anyone is in Christ, he is a new creation. The old order has passed away; now all is new!" (2 Cor 5:17).

Far from impeding the dynamic elan toward the future, the present possessed by hope gives it added impetus. It makes possible the realization in time of the newness brought by the risen Christ. This is demonstrated in the Person and action of the Holy Spirit.

The Pledge of the Spirit

The beginning of fulfillment that characterizes Christian hope comes to it from the Holy Spirit, "the pledge of our inheritance" (Ep 1:14), in whom we were sealed through baptism (cf. Ep 1:13). The divine inheritance, namely, all that belongs to the Father and that is shared by the Son, is given us in the Holy Spirit as a "first payment" (Ep 1:14).

Saint Paul says the Spirit has been promised (cf. Ep 1:13). In the Acts of the Apostles the Spirit is designated in a still more telling way as the Father's promise (cf. Ac 1:4). When Jesus told his disciples not to leave Jerusalem, but to await the coming of the Holy Spirit, he did not refer to him by name but as the One promised by the Father. In the Spirit is the total divine gift announced in the Old Testament. That is why the coming of the Holy Spirit was the fulfillment of ancient hopes. The time of the promise had passed, and the age of fulfillment had arrived. Admittedly, it was not yet total fulfillment, but only the "first payment" on the divine inheritance. Still, this beginning of possession was of the same divine nature as the ultimate consummation.

In other words, the whole of Christian hope is concentrated in the Holy Spirit, both as possessed and as impelled toward the final goal.

However, we may wonder whether the identification of hope with the Holy Spirit is compatible with the identification of hope with Christ. If hope has already been

concentrated in Christ, is it not superfluous to attribute
to the Holy Spirit the role of concentrating all Christian
hope within himself? How can these two statements be
reconciled?

Christ himself invited his disciples to put all their
hope in the Holy Spirit. For when he told them to await
his coming, he announced they would receive a power
from the Spirit that would enable them to carry out their
mission as witnesses "even to the ends of the earth" (Acts
1:8).

Already in John's Gospel we learn that Jesus' promises so filled with hope are to be understood as referring
to the Spirit. "But whoever drinks the water I give him
will never be thirsty; no, the water I give shall become
a fountain within him, leaping up to provide eternal life"
(Jn 4:14). "If anyone thirsts, let him come to me; let him
drink who believes in me. Scripture has it: 'From within
him rivers of living water shall flow.' (Here he was referring to the Spirit, whom those that came to believe
in him were to receive. There was, of course, no Spirit
as yet, since Jesus had not yet been glorified.)" (Jn 7:37-
39). It is the glorious Christ whose role it is to pour out
the Spirit. John attached great significance to the lance
thrust, because he saw the shedding of the blood and the
water as a symbol of the pouring out of the Holy Spirit,
as the sign of the rivers of living water that were beginning to flow (cf. Jn 19:34).

The Holy Spirit is therefore Jesus' gift to his disciples,
the fruit of the redemptive sacrifice that, once he had
attained his glory, he communicated to those he had come
to save. That is why the Holy Spirit is the totality of
Christian hope. By reason of the fact that Christ is our
hope, the Spirit given by him realizes the content of hope.
The glorious Christ gives men life in his Spirit, and
through the Spirit the Father gives mankind life in
Christ. "If the Spirit of him who raised Jesus from the

dead dwells in you, then he who raised Christ from the
dead will bring your mortal bodies to life also, through
his Spirit dwelling in you" (Rm 8:11).

Paul is not content to indicate the future effect to be
accomplished by the Spirit, namely, the gift of life to
mortal bodies. He affirms that the Spirit dwells in us
here and now. This indwelling is so real and permeates
the flesh so completely that Christians, and their bodies
in particular, become sanctuaries. "You must know that
your body is a temple of the Holy Spirit, who is within—
the Spirit you have received from God" (1 Cor 6:19; cf.
3:16-17).

The risen Christ influences men by communicating
the Holy Spirit to them. This is because his Resurrection
was accomplished in the Spirit, involving a spiritual
transformation of his physical being. As a result, Christ
makes the Holy Spirit dwell within us, as he already
dwells within him.

And so there is no opposition or dichotomy between
the presence of the glorious Christ and the presence of
the Holy Spirit. They both personify our hope. In the
event of the Redemption, Christ summed up all hope in
himself in a more objective way. Through the Spirit, new
hope springs up within us in a subjective way. The glorious Christ communicates himself to believers through
the Spirit. The Spirit, for his part, is in a more immediate
way the gift and the communication. Hence, to possess
the Spirit is to possess hope.

The Spirit, Hope of Total Truth

There is no clearer expression of the complementary
role of the Holy Spirit in relation to Christ's than Jesus'
own statements during his discourse after the Last

Supper: "I will ask the Father and he will give you another Paraclete—to be with you always: the Spirit of truth, whom the world cannot accept, since it neither sees him nor recognizes him; but you can recognize him because he remains with you and will be within you" (Jn 14:16-17).

The words "another Paraclete" indicate that the Holy Spirit was to have a role similar to that of Jesus, the role of a defender or intercessor. He was to remain in the disciples, just as Christ said he would. Like Christ, too, who said "I am the truth," he is "the Spirit of truth."

The specific mission of the Holy Spirit is also expressed by Jesus' promise: "the Paraclete, the Holy Spirit whom the Father will send in my name, will instruct you in everything, and remind you of all that I told you" (Jn 14:26). Jesus had brought men the supreme revelation. His life and his message told the whole truth. "I have made known to you all that I heard from my Father" (Jn 15:15). The revelation was now complete, but it still had to be accepted by the disciples. Those who had listened to Jesus needed someone to remind them of all he had said to them.

More specifically, Jesus declared: "I have much more to tell you, but you cannot bear it now. When he comes, however, being the Spirit of truth he will guide you to all truth. He will not speak on his own, but will speak only what he hears, and will announce to you the things to come. In doing this he will give glory to me, because he will have received from me what he will announce to you" (Jn 16:12-14).

When we read this text we might have the impression that it does not agree with the preceding one. Here the role of the Holy Spirit consists in saying what Jesus was unable to say, whereas in the earlier passage his role is to remind the disciples of everything Jesus has said. Actually there is no conflict between the two declarations. They simply express different points of view. The former stresses the identity between the teaching of the Holy Spirit and that of Jesus. The latter emphasizes the newness of the Holy Spirit's input.

To say that the Holy Spirit will guide us "to all truth" is to call to mind everything Jesus has said as well as the many things he still had to say but which his disciples were not able to bear at that time. These many things are not truths to be added, but include everything about Jesus' message that the disciples had been unable to grasp when he gave it. Jesus remains the total revelation, the revelation to which nothing was lacking, but a revelation that could not be fully understood by those to whom it was addressed. To the Holy Spirit devolved the task of unveiling the meaning of this revelation and opening minds to this meaning. While this is essentially a task of transmission and interpretation, it involves a new input because there are still many discoveries to make about the mystery revealed by Christ.

Here we find once again the characteristic mark of hope, implying at once possession in the present moment and newness in subsequent developments. Truth is already possessed, but it still remains to be explored so as to increase knowledge and show the way to new interpretations. The Holy Spirit makes us perceive this newness by constantly inspiring new intellectual efforts, but always within the message brought by Christ.

Thus, our hope to know revealed truth, that is, the essential truth concerning God, concerning man, and their mutual relations, rests in the Holy Spirit. We must never forget that Jesus insisted on the totality of the truth the Spirit was to unveil to us: "he will guide you to **all truth**," "he . . . will announce to you **the things to come**" (Jn 16:13). And so there must be no limitation to our hope of better understanding God's plan for the world and for us. Besides, the reason Jesus spoke to us about "the Spirit of truth" was to awaken in us the desire to receive this truth, and to encourage us to hope for a more complete knowledge of the universe of grace.

This total truth is summed up in Christ. Jesus says of the Holy Spirit: "he will give glory to me" (Jn 16:14). The truth the Spirit communicates to us comes from Jesus: "because he will have received from me what he will announce to you" (Jn 16:14). And finally this truth relates to Jesus. "When the Paraclete comes, the Spirit of truth who comes from the Father—and whom I myself will send from the Father—he will bear witness on my behalf" (Jn 15:26). More particularly, through the transformation brought about in the disciples, the Spirit manifests the Savior's divine power and identity.

The event of Pentecost confirmed this role of witnessing. At the conclusion of what had just happened, Peter declared that Jesus "first received the promised Holy Spirit from the Father, then poured this Spirit out on us" (Ac 2:33), as proof of his Resurrection and Ascension. "Therefore," Peter went on, "let the whole house of Israel know beyond any doubt that God has made both Lord and Messiah this Jesus whom you crucified" (Ac 2:36).

This episode also shows how the witness of the Holy Spirit concerning Jesus is the source of the Apostles' witness. After declaring that the Spirit of truth would bear witness to him, Jesus announced: "You must bear witness as well . . ." (Jn 15:27). And Peter affirmed the same thing in his discourse on Pentecost: "This is the Jesus God has raised up, and we are his witnesses" (Ac 2:32).

In guiding men toward the total truth, the Holy Spirit wants to inspire this witness, for the truth he discloses is destined to take possession of the whole of human existence. To proclaim the truth communicated to us in Christ is to make it the wellspring of a more abundant human life and to transmit it as a message to be shared with others.

The Holy Spirit is the hope of a truth that can transform the whole life of man.

The Spirit, Hope of Love

Saint Paul said to the Romans: "And this hope will not leave us disappointed, because the love of God has been poured out in our hearts through the Holy Spirit who has been given to us" (Rm 5:5). He was referring to the love God showed in our regard in the drama of the Redemption: "It is precisely in this that God proves his love for us: that while we were still sinners, Christ died for us" (Rm 5:8).

God's love could have remained beyond the reach of mankind. Even though this love consisted in giving his Son to be sacrificed for our salvation, it would have remained God's own property, remote and unapproachable. Had that been the case, our hope could have been threatened. But inasmuch as this love has been incorporated into our human life and dwells in us through the Holy Spirit, hope cannot disappoint us.[7] For, in the Spirit, our hope possesses divine love and can never be separated from this love again.

Here we find the basis for the hymn to hope that follows in the same Letter of Paul: "Who will separate us from the love of Christ? Trial, or distress, or persecution, or hunger, or nakedness, or danger, or the sword? As Scripture says: 'For your sake we are being slain all the day long; we are looked upon as sheep to be slaughtered' (Ps 44:23). Yet in all this we are more than conquerors because of him who has loved us. For I am certain that neither death nor life, neither angels nor principalities, neither the present nor the future, nor powers, neither height nor depth nor any other creature, will be able to separate us from the love of God that comes to us in Christ Jesus, our Lord" (Rm 8:35-39).

The reason we cannot be separated from God's love is that it has entered our hearts through the gift of the Spirit. Hope is not to be confounded because it rests on this inward reality.[8]

Besides, when divine love penetrates deep into human hearts, it transforms them and establishes them in a permanent attitude of charity. The Holy Spirit is not received in a passive way only. He is also the active principle of attitudes of love.

First of all, the Holy Spirit inspires an attitude of filial love for the Father: "All who are led by the Spirit of God are sons of God. You did not receive a spirit of slavery leading you back into fear, but a spirit of adoption through which we cry out 'Abba!' (that is, 'Father'). The Spirit himself gives witness with our spirit that we are children of God" (Rm 8:14-16). "The proof that you are sons is the fact that God has sent forth into our hearts the spirit of his Son which cries out 'Abba!' ('Father!')" (Gal 4:6). This cry "Father!", which expresses the closest possible intimacy with the Father, contains all possible hope of trusting relations with God. From the fact that the Holy Spirit comes within us as the Spirit of love, he cannot incite sentiments of fear. He ends religious slavery and gives the freedom of sons, thereby eliminating some terrifying obstacles to hope. We remember how Kierkegaard was driven to despair by his dread of God, an anguished fear he could never completely overcome and that he had discovered in his father's Christianity. Such a sentiment does not come from the Holy Spirit given to the Christian.

In addition, the Spirit nurtures love for neighbor. He implants in the Christian's behavior God's own love for men. We find this truth triumphantly expressed in John's First Epistle: "Beloved, if God has loved us so, we must have the same love for one another. . . . if we love one another God dwells in us, and his love is brought to perfection in us. The way we know we remain in him and he in us is that he has given us of his Spirit" (I Jn 4:11-13).

Hope is especially necessary in the area of generous and constant relationships of love with our neighbor. It is no easy task to maintain such relationships, as we all know from our everyday experience. Once the Christian has been taught the all-important command of charity, he does not rely on his own strength to obey it. He depends on the power of the Holy Spirit who enables him to love after the example of Christ, breaking through all the restraints human egoism would place on self-giving. The presence of the Holy Spirit gives the Christian the assurance that even in the most arduous circumstances he will be able to maintain and increase his love for his neighbor.

Pentecost, an Explosion of Hope

There was a flagrant disproportion between the mission to bear witness to Christ to the ends of the earth and the paltry human resources of the small group of disciples that had clustered around the Master. They might well have deemed such a far-flung mission impossible, and given in to discouragement, even despair. What made the mission seem all the more overpowering was that Jesus had not given it to his disciples until he was about to leave them permanently. If he had remained on earth he could easily have inspired those who had begun to believe in him before his death to follow him in his glory. His miracles had demonstrated he had a divine power that could laugh at human impossibilities. The disciples could have counted on this omnipotence to sustain them in spreading the Gospel throughout the world. Jesus' departure put an end to such hopes. After the Ascension the disciples found themselves totally unprepared for their mission.

Of course, Jesus had told them that his departure would benefit them: "I tell you the sober truth: It is much better for you that I go. If I fail to go, the Paraclete will never come to you, whereas if I go, I will send him to you" (Jn 16:7). But those who had heard these words were not prepared to grasp their meaning. After several years of close fellowship with Christ in whom they had put all their trust for the future, they could not understand how they could benefit from being separated from him. The announced "Paraclete" was very mysterious to them, and his coming, they thought, could not compensate for the absence of the Master to whom they had vowed their lives.

So Jesus' Ascension left the disciples disheartened, but it also inspired them to prayer. Aware of their human weakness in the face of a mission far beyond their capacities, they had no other recourse but prayer sustained by their anticipation of the "fulfillment of [the] Father's promise" (Ac 1:4).

In response to the disciples' unanimous and untiring prayer (Ac 1:14), Pentecost far exceeded their expectations. The violence of the event indicates that God intended to produce profound changes in the assembled disciples. The strong wind symbolizes the powerful inspiration that took hold of the entire community and of each of its members. It was as though the Holy Spirit wanted to bring forth new personalities.

Was Pentecost really an explosion of hope? It was that and more. First of all, it involved the transformation of the disciples who were now filled with zeal to witness to God's mighty deeds. This transformation in turn filled them with a vast new hope that swept them into far-reaching apostolic adventures.

The mood of dejection and retreat gave way to a pervading joy in their new mission. Pentecost gave direction to their vision and actions. Their horizons were no longer limited to the past, to a remembrance of Christ, dead and risen. Their eyes were turned toward a future to be built through the divine power of Christ who had sent his Spirit to them.

And so it is with Christianity today. It cannot focus on its past, but must continually advance boldly toward future progress. It cannot limit its goal to defending itself against encircling enemies after the manner of the first Christian community before Pentecost. It must seek to reach heights so far unattained.

This gives us a glimpse of the unlimited horizons of hope. From the very beginning, the Church appealed to a gathering of people who represented every nation and tongue.[9] At Pentecost the worldwide witness that Jesus had proposed to his disciples was set in motion. It was a pledge of the future in the present. In the end, no human frontiers will stop the forward march of the Christian community or counter the ambitions of Christian hope.

NOTES FOR CHAPTER SIX

1. Cf. Moltmann, **Théologie de l'espérance**, pp. 39, 165.

2. The Epistle to the Thessalonians already expressed the object of hope in terms of union with Christ, (I Thes. 5:10). Cf. G. Didier, **Désintéressement du chrétien. La rétribution dans la morale de saint Paul**, Paris, 1955, pp. 35-36, with a critical note on the interpretation given by J. Dupont, **Sun Christo, l'union avec le Christ selon saint Paul, I, Avec le Christ dans la vie future**, Bruges-Louvain, 1953.

3. This is Moltmann's answer, op. cit., pp. 29 ff.

4. We should not give too absolute a meaning to the distinction St. Augustine makes between "hope" and "reality," as in the following passage: "cum credimus, spes est in saeculo; cum videbimus, res erit in futuro saeculo," (**En. in Ps**. 123:2; CCL 40, 1826; cf. U. Occhialini, **La speranza della Chiesa pellegrina**, Assisi, 1965, pp. 66-73). The distinction has a lovely sound in Latin: **spes - res**, but it must not be understood as if hope did not yet contain anything of the hoped-for reality. Elsewhere St. Augustine uses the comparison of the egg (**Sermo** 105, 7; PL 38, 621).

5. Op. cit., p. 27.

6. Moltmann thinks that Christ rose from the dead not in the Spirit and the kerygma, but in a still undetermined vestibule to the future, to which the impetus of the Spirit and the announcements of the kerygma point, (cf. op. cit., p. 227). The New Testament shows us, on the contrary, that Christ rose in the Spirit. Cf. in particular, F. X. Durrwell, C.SS.R., **The Resurrection, a Biblical Study**, (Sheed & Ward, 1960), "Christ Raised by the Spirit," pp. 91ff.

7. The verb Paul uses means not only "disappoint" but also "confound" with a nuance of disgrace (cf. Spicq, **Agapè dans le Nouveau Testament**, II, pp. 173ff.)

8. To possess God's love is to possess "something of the nature or of the very life of God," says Spicq (**ibid.**, p. 179). "Of the nature" is less direct, for we are speaking of a freely given, unearned divine love. "Of the life" is more immediate, for to have the love of God within us is to possess God's own life.

9. In his commentary on Pentecost, J. Dupont concludes with these words on the presence of people from all nations: "The Church was born universal.... That is the essential meaning of the miracle of Pentecost. The Spirit gave the whole world to the Church, obliging it by that very fact to engage in an enormous missionary effort through which it would attain its plenitude and eschatological stature" (**Etudes sur les Actes des Apôtres**, p. 501). Here we grasp the nature of hope: the universalism of the Church has not yet been realized in fact; yet it is entirely present in Christian hope. Hope implies what will be in what already is.

CHAPTER VII

HOPE IN THE
MYSTERY OF THE CHURCH

True and False Hope

As Jesus was giving his disciples his last commands before his Ascension, he was asked this question: "Lord, are you going to restore the rule to Israel now?" (Ac 1:6). Realizing their Master's departure was imminent, the disciples expressed the substance of all their expectations, their hope of a Messiah.

In his response Jesus sought to make them understand what was wrong with such a hope and to inspire them with authentic hope.

Luke tells us that during the preceding forty days Jesus spoke to them "about the reign of God" (Acts 1:3). He had already told them that his kingdom was not of this world (cf. Jn 18:36),[1] and clearly demonstrated it by holding Peter back when he wanted to use his sword to defend him against his enemies (cf. Jn 18:11). Yet in spite of all this the disciples could not throw off their traditional notions of a political kingdom. Since they had not understood the meaning of the Paschal mystery they continued to hope that Jesus would launch a campaign to restore the sovereignty of the Jewish people, lost since the beginning of the Roman occupation. They stubbornly insisted on confusing God's realm with Caesar's.

Jesus answered that the kingdom would grow through

their witness and not by force of arms, and he stressed the universality of this witness which, far from being limited to the Jewish people, would reach "even to the ends of the earth" (Ac 1:8). His warning was to retain its value for all Christian generations, for the temptation of the "kingdom of Israel" would continue throughout the history of the Church. Some have been inclined to identify the kingdom of Christ with a political kingdom, a social class, a race, a nation. It is hard to admit unequivocally that Christ's kingdom is God's, above all the particularisms that divide human society. Hope thus always faces the danger of going astray, of aspiring to political positions for the Church, and power like that of political states.

The disciples' second delusion was to think that the kingdom could be restored quickly: "now." Jesus answered that it would take a long time. "The exact time it is not yours to know. The Father has reserved that to himself" (Ac 1:7). The kingdom was to develop in successive stages, according to the Father's infallible decrees.

Christian hope has been invited to accept the slow pace of this development. Its eagerness must never lead it to think that it can be achieved in one fell swoop. Men would prefer to think the Church has already attained its perfect development, that its universality in fact coincides with its universality by right, that is to say, with the whole world. For its mission is to make Christ known by all mankind. However, the course of history, as the Father has outlined it, is not so swift.

A third strand of the disciples' hope did not conform to the divine plan. They kept asking Jesus when he was finally going to begin to act. They didn't realize that through the Paschal mystery Jesus had completed his work and henceforth it was their task to labor for the kingdom. In answer to the question: "Lord, are you going to restore the rule to Israel?" Jesus answered: "You are to be my witnesses." Now that Jesus was leaving this earth, the disciples were to assure his presence by their own personal lives. They were to assume responsibility for the kingdom.

That is why authentic Christian hope involves commitment to the work begun by Christ. It demands the gift of self in witnessing, with the use of all one's talents and resources to spread the Gospel message. While the Christian well knows that everything is in the Father's hands, he realizes he himself must contribute to the coming of the kingdom.

It is in this light we must understand the words the angels spoke to the disciples after Jesus had disappeared from their sight: "Men of Galilee, why do you stand here looking up at the skies? This Jesus who has been taken from you will return, just as you saw him go up into the heavens" (Ac 1:11). There is question here of a coming similar but not identical to the departure. The reference is not to the Parousia, but to the great Messianic coming to occur in the development of the kingdom upon earth. This coming would result from a corporeal departure, for it was a coming according to the Spirit.

That is why the angels urged the disciples not to stand there gazing up to heaven, as if Jesus were about to descend again from the skies. They were to look at the earth, where the coming of Christ would be accomplished. And as this was to be a spiritual coming, they were to cooperate in it by their witness. By accepting Jesus' bodily departure, they would be able to contribute to his spiritual coming. It was a call to apostolic work.

True hope is directed toward the coming of Christ in his Church, a completely real coming, and one whose fruit and manifestation will be the final Parousia.

Hope for the Progress of the Church

When Jesus gave his disciples the mission to bear witness "even to the ends of the earth" and to teach all nations, he was asking them to hope for the development of the Church.

He had already briefly outlined this development in his eschatological discourse. The imminent disaster, by which he meant his Passion, would not coincide with the end of the world, and would be only "the onset of the pains of labor" (Mk 13:8), the beginning of a time of suffering when the disciples in their turn would undergo persecution, need to resist the enticements of false prophets, and keep their love from growing cold under the assaults of evil. "This good news of the kingdom will be proclaimed throughout the world as a witness to all the nations. Only after that will the end come" (Mt 24:14). So the Church is to develop amid trials and labor pains, in the face of hostility and attacks by the forces of evil, meanwhile extending its influence over the whole world. Only when the Church completes this task will the end come.

Jesus presented a vision of the end of the world very different from any the disciples could have had. The end will not be a disaster that will suddenly interrupt the course of history and hurl the world into a frightful catastrophe. Rather, it will be the consummation of the world's destiny through the work of the Church. Once the Gospel has penetrated the whole world, history will come to an end because the universe will have attained its goal.

In commenting on the mystery of the development of the Church among the pagans, Paul indicates that the Jews' recalcitrance to accept the Gospel has favored its acceptance by other nations, but is also preparing the way for an even greater manifestation of divine mercy in the granting of salvation.

"Brothers, I do not want you to be ignorant of this mystery lest you be conceited: blindness has come upon part of Israel until the full number of Gentiles enter in, and then all of Israel will be saved. As Scripture says: 'Out of Zion will come the deliverer . . .' " (Rm 11:25-26). All the peoples of the world are destined to "enter in," to take their places in the kingdom, and finally Israel after the pagans.[2]

Paul interpreted in the fullest sense Jesus' declarations on the proclamation of the good news to all nations. The preaching of the Gospel throughout the world will not suffice to herald the coming of the end. More will be required. The Gospel will first have to penetrate the world and the "pleroma" or total aggregate of the nations will have to accept it and enter into the kingdom.

We must not conclude from this that a time will come when all individuals will have entered the Church.[3] Jesus amply warned his disciples of the hostility that would pursue them. There will always be enemies of the kingdom. Opposition to the Gospel will not cease, and the growth of the Christian community will involve bitter struggles. But the Church is moving toward a final stage when it will embrace the totality of nations.

We do not know what the phases of this progressive expansion of the Church will be, since only the Father knows "the exact day or hour" (Mt 24:36) and he "has reserved that to himself" (Ac 1:7).[4]

History demonstrates that there are "hours of grace" for nations as well as individuals. There are moments when the preaching of the Gospel finds fertile soil among certain peoples and the Church extends its influence very rapidly, while in other lands the moment has not yet come to welcome its message.

We likewise do not know how long it will take to bring this development to completion. The Father alone will decide the date of the end of the world,[5] and Jesus has given us to understand that we shall not be told what that date is.

The experience of the Church tells us only that the delay will be much longer than the first Christians had expected. At the start of his apostolic ministry Paul hoped still to be alive at the moment of the Parousia. But the further he got into his work of preaching the better he realized that the conversion of all nations would require much more time. The current explosion of the world's population seems to indicate it will take a very long time, centuries or perhaps millenia, before the whole of mankind finds its way into the Church.

We should not deduce that the Church will always remain a minority group in the world because of its slow development characterized by moments of ebb and flow. Trust in Christ's word bolsters the Christian hope with the certitude that the future of the human race belongs to the Church. Time and history make possible the progressive diffusion of Christ's grace throughout the human community.

Progress is not limited to expansion in space. The work of penetrating mankind with grace also involves progress in depth and hence in quality. As the Christian community develops it lives ever more completely by Christ's holiness. Faith, hope, and love never cease growing within the Church.

We should be warned against the myth of an ideal primitive community, of a Church that might have experienced a golden age from the start. This would imply that subsequent history has been a kind of decadence from the high degree of perfection enjoyed in the beginning. As a matter of fact, Paul's statements in his Epistles castigating the members of the first Christian communities suffice to show that such an idyllic state never existed.

In a general way, we must avoid idealizing the past and not yield to our impressions of a contemporary decadence.

Despite crises and periods of regression, the general trend of the Church has been upward. The most recent history confirms this. For example, Vatican Council II has certainly given evidence of new progress in charity, especially in the area of ecumenism, relations with other religions, and respect for the individual conscience.

Awareness of the current faults of the Christian community, among members of the hierarchy as well as the laity, should not, therefore, be an impediment to hope rightly placed in the Church. Not only has this Church received from Christ the assurance that it would not succumb to the powers of evil (Mt 16:18), it has always been led by the Holy Spirit toward progress and growth, impelling it to combat and overcome its imperfections. The Church knows very well it is not perfect, since it is still a society of sinners, but in tending toward perfection it uplifts the level of morality of all mankind.

The law of progress likewise indicates that the Christian community can never stop and take a rest, or feel satisfied with the results already achieved. The hope of ever greater perfection continually stimulates the Church to outstrip its current phase of development.

The Hope of the Universe

Paul tells us the universe joins in our hope. "Indeed, the whole created world eagerly awaits the revelation of the sons of God. Creation was made subject to futility, not of its own accord but by him who once subjected it; yet not without hope, because the world itself will be freed from its slavery to corruption and share in the glorious freedom of the children of God. Yes, we know

that all creation groans and is in agony even until now"
(Rm 8:19-21).

God's plan of salvation concerns the entire universe.
That means that Christian hope embraces physical as
well as spiritual realities.[6]

As for Christians, their hope is addressed above all
to the salvation that is being prepared for their bodies.
". . . we ourselves, although we have the Spirit as first
fruits, groan inwardly while we await the redemption of
our bodies" (Rm 8:22).[7]

Hope, we see, assumes cosmic proportions. It embraces
the entire visible world. This raises the problem of the
integration of earthly values into Christian hope. In
earlier times hope often found expression in a scorn for
earthly things and an exclusive desire for heavenly joys.
Today by virtue of a contrary reaction, the emphasis is
often on the necessity of including the temporal development of mankind within the notion of hope.

This problem deserves to be discussed at much greater
length. We shall limit ourselves here to a few affirmations
of principle that will help to throw light on individual
applications.

First of all, nothing can be considered foreign to
Christian hope. There is no aspect of human life, no
material being, outside the scope of hope.[8] Not only is
everything about the created world worthy of respect,
but it is also included in the sphere of influence embraced by divine salvation.

Moreover, the material universe has not been endowed with its own special kind of hope, cut off from
the hope that sustains mankind. The hope of the material
world is to "share in the glorious freedom of the children
of God" (Rm 8:21). Indeed, it was created to help man
achieve his destiny. In consequence, it has shared the
fate of men subjected to sin's yoke and shares equally
in their salvation.

The hope of the material world is entirely directed toward man. In particular it must share in man's ultimate corporeal transformation, in "the redemption of our bodies" (Rm 8:23) for which we hope. The material world is truly bound up with man's physical body. Thus, the resurrection of the body will be accompanied by a transformation of the material universe which will then share the divine life of the spiritual world.

By reason of the fact that the entire cosmos is included within the perspectives of hope, the Christian cannot be indifferent to activities addressed to earthly goals. He must even become more deeply involved in them, realizing that through these earthly values he is building a world completely integrated into the eternal life conferred on mankind. That is why he must contribute to the material well-being and cultural development of humanity and is called upon, according to his talents and capabilities, to encourage social progress, science, and art in all its forms; in short, to promote the diffusion of the values of civilization.

At the same time, the Christian's hope does not stop at these earthly values considered in themselves. He retains his supernatural perspective, for the definitive measure of these values is the degree of love they express, love of God and love of neighbor. If earthly values failed to make the world better in view of its authentic destiny or failed to contribute to the advent of a more loving human society, they would be diverted from their deepest purpose, which is to be incorporated into the plan of salvation.

This same supernatural perspective helps us to see that the promotion of earthly values can never culminate in a hope for some sort of earthly paradise. The presence of the cross is inevitable and must be acknowledged. We have already pointed out the essential role of the Paschal mystery in Christian hope. Trials open the door to deeper joy, and the passage from the Passion to the Resurrection is a fundamental law of Christian life. Sufferings, failures, physical and psychological impairment take on meaning when seen in this light. They are seen to be ordered to the development of man's most fundamental values.

Personal Hope and Communitarian Hope

For too long, a sector of Christian education has focussed on developing an individualistic hope. Witness the "acts of hope" whose object was simply to attain personal happiness in the world beyond and to obtain the graces necessary to this end. By a curious paradox, the "act of hope" that was the pendant to the "act of charity" lacked charity. It tended to make the Christian concentrate on his own individual destiny and taught him to act only for his own best interests.

Authentic Christian hope is communitarian. We should remember that the hope expressed in the Old Testament was also essentially communitarian, for it was concerned with the future of the Jewish people. Far from losing this community-awareness, Christian hope has expanded and deepened it. It expanded it by extending its aspirations to all mankind. It deepened it because the Christian community was formed at a greater depth, being assembled in the unity of Christ and in the bond of charity that unites all those who follow him. In this unity it is impossible for the Christian to separate himself from his brothers when he hopes. He can only hope with them and for them.

Pentecost manifested the communitarian aspect of hope in a special way. The gift of the Holy Spirit was poured out upon the community. It was within this community that Christian hope was born, and it was to this community that Christian hope was permanently entrusted. All those who were incorporated into the Church in later centuries were joined to its hope as well as to its faith and love. A Christian does not create his own hope. He shares a hope that is the possession of the Church. It is the Church that hopes within each of its members.

This does not mean individual hope is thereby weakened or eliminated. The community does not abolish persons, nor is it formed at their expense. Rather, the community needs all the individual riches of each of its members. The blossoming of a communitarian hope thus harmonizes with the development of personal hope. The Christian places his hope in his individual destiny as it has been decreed in the divine plan of salvation. In the words of Saint Paul, he believes he has been chosen by the Father from the creation of the world through a loving predestination, to be holy and blameless in his sight and to become his adopted child in Jesus (cf. Ep 1:3-5). He hopes for the happiness of ultimate reunion with Christ beyond death. He is aware of possessing the gift of the Holy Spirit which implants an eternal life within him here and now, and he is sure of the divine covenant that sustains him in difficult moments and enables him to overcome the obstacles to his salvation.

This personal hope is a great source of strength especially in the Christian's apostolic mission. He knows he has been called to bear witness to Christ, to spread the Gospel's message. In the power of the Spirit, he hopes his Christian life will bear much fruit. Even when he cannot discern any visible results he has the inner certitude that each of his efforts to follow Christ, to grow in love and make the world better will benefit others. Convinced of the solidarity that unites him to all his brothers and sisters, he knows everything he does has value for the Church.

The apostolic dimension of Christian living reveals the integration of personal hope in communitarian hope. The ultimate goal of hope is the gathering of all mankind in an eternal community of happiness at the end of the world. The more immediate goal is the present-day development of the Church, its expansion throughout the world and its growth in love, in preparation for the final state of completion.

Christian hope is absolutely certain of fulfillment as to its general goals, but certitude does not make this hope useless. For hope is the cooperation demanded of men in the Father's power for the development of the kingdom. Christian hope can hasten the final denouement by stimulating the spread of the Church over the world and its growth in holiness.

Through this communitarian hope, the Christian enters the stream of human history and helps to orientate history toward its supreme goal. He fulfills his personal responsibility in achieving the world's completion.

NOTES FOR CHAPTER SEVEN

1. It is interesting to note that John's formulation "of this world" stresses the spatial milieu rather than the time factor, as in the Synoptic formulation (cf. Barrett, St. John, p. 447). The kingdom belongs less to another time than to another spirit or level of life.

2. There is more than a chronological link between the two phases. There is also a causal link expressed by "and then" which means "and as a result" (cf. M. J. Lagrange, Epître aux Romains, Paris, 1950, p. 284).

3. As Lagrange remarks (ibid.): "This plenitude is to be understood of the nations and not of individual persons. All the nations will be converted to Christ, but not necessarily all the individuals of the Gentile nations."

4. The two Greek terms are not identical. Chronos means time that has duration; kairos, a propitious instant. Cf. E. des Places, Tempora vel momenta (Ac. 1:7; cf. Ac. 17:26 and 30; Mélanges E. Tisserant, I, Studi e Testi 231, Rome, 1964, pp. 105-117). The translation might be: "delays or favorable moments." Acts 17:26 and 30 bring out the distinction between moments of salvation and periods of ignorance.

5. J. Winandy has pointed out the sense of the text: " 'the exact day or hour' that 'the Father has reserved . . . to himself' does not mean that the Father has fixed them by his own authority, but that the Father has reserved to himself the personal decision on the matter. The moment is not yet fixed because it likewise depends on human freedom, on man's acceptance of salvation. It is reserved for the Father to determine the moment" (cf. "Le logion de l'ignorance Mk. 13:32; Mt. 24:36," Revue Biblique 75, (1968), pp. 76-79).

6. This creation is in store for the universe, without excluding human beings (cf. Kuss, Römerbrief, II, p. 624; A. Viard, "Expectatio creaturae (Rm. 8:19-22)," Revue Biblique 59, (1952), pp. 337-359). According to Paul's text, creation is offered as a parallel and does not refer to Christians per se.

7. On the text of the verse and the omission of the term "filial adoption," cf. P. Benoît, "We . . . groan inwardly while we await the redemption of our bodies" (Rm. 8:23), Mélanges Lebreton, I, Recherches de Science Religieuse 39, (1951-52). pp. 267-280.

8. We wonder whether Occhialini correctly expresses St. Augustine's thought when he says that, for Augustine, to hope for temporal goods is a sinful act (La speranza, p. 103). According to the texts, Augustine condemns such hope only in the measure that it is directed exclusively to these temporal goods. Cf. P. Delahaye-J. Boulangé, Espérance de vie chrétienne, Tournai, 1958, p. 120. In Augustine's commentary on the Lord's prayer, the petitions point out the objects of our hope, and among them are temporal goods ordered to eternal life (Enchiridion de fide, spe et caritate, edited by J. Rivière, Bibliothèque Augustinienne, Vol. 9, Paris, 1947, XXX, pp. 114-116).

CHAPTER VIII

HOPE IN THE LIFE OF A CHRISTIAN

The Christian, A Man of Hope

A Christian can be defined as a man of hope. Evidently this is not the only possible definition. A Christian might be defined with equal accuracy as a man of faith or a man of love, for faith and love, like hope, govern the totality of the Christian life.

Hope should suffice to set the Christian apart, because hope implies a vision of a world dominated by the work of divine salvation, together with the perseverance needed to help bring this work to completion. Hope encompasses the whole of the truth to be believed, seeing in it the future it offers mankind. Likewise, hope embraces the whole of life and motivates all action, because it turns the Christian not only toward the world beyond death but also toward the progress of the Church in this world. Through hope the Christian commits himself to share in the mission of the Christian community, with all his powers of action, thought, and feeling. Before the future can become a reality, it must be present through hope in the Christian's heart.

A good way to find out what is in a man is to ask him what his hopes are. In a person's hopes can be found the deepest motives for his actions. We should not judge anyone solely on what he is now or on what he has done up until this moment. Through hope he can burst out of the limitations that have fettered him and survive crushing trials. The person who firmly expects a better future and is striving with all his being to attain it gradually takes on the dimensions of this future.

What is true of all human beings is true in a more special way of the Christian. Deep within him, he already possesses in a certain measure a future that exceeds the present. It is his vocation to live in expectation of this future. He would be repudiating what he is were he not to aspire to a better world, both here on earth and in the life beyond.

The Church, like the individual Christian, deserves to be judged not only on the basis of its witness and influence within contemporary society, but still more by the hope rooted in it. This hope is part and parcel of the reality of the Church. It is a spiritual treasure of the highest order, as well as a precious contribution to the progress of mankind. The Church proposes to the world the ideal of perfect love, believes in this ideal, and makes others believe in it as a permanent condition of the human community, to be fully achieved only after death but constantly progressing on earth. This alone is a remarkable service that would justify the Church's existence.

When we define the Christian, and the Church itself for that matter, in terms of hope, we are contradicting those who are far too engrossed with Christianity's origins. The Christian religion has too often been seen as a religion of the past, governed by rigorous conformity to primordial laws and traditions. It thus appeared to abhor innovation, to dread new historical situations, as well as new trends of thought that captivate men's minds.

Hope reveals the Church with greater truth. While it does not disregard the essential role of fidelity to the past, it manifests the elan and power for innovation inherent in the Church's equally fundamental concern with the future.

The Church lives by a Revelation and Redemption already accomplished in Christ, but in view of building a new world. We must learn to discern the profound dynamism that impels the Church boldly onward in its task.

Hope makes the individual Christian understand the ultimate meaning of his life and efforts. It opens to him exciting perspectives on the religion he professes. It invites him to overcome the disappointments of his own life, to welcome unexpected change and renewal, and helps him to achieve total personal fulfillment.

Hope, Fountain of Life

In the Old Testament the object of hope, both personal and collective, was a more abundant and happier life.[1] It was rooted in the most fundamental human drive: the will to live. And this meant the will to prolong one's life, to overcome all obstacles, to live happily, and to multiply one's life through a large posterity which pushed back life's frontiers indefinitely in time as well as space.

Men realized they were powerless to attain such a life by themselves and sought it from God.

Christian hope is founded on the risen Christ who relates it to the surge of a new life of the spirit. For a Christian, to hope is to seek to live Christ's own life in plenitude, and it is to begin living this life now.

The Father "gave us a new birth; a birth unto hope which draws its life from the resurrection of Jesus Christ from the dead" (1 P 1:3). This new birth brings forth the Christian to life and hope. Life is hope, because it looks to the future, and hope is life because the new birth has already occurred.

As this is a divine, eternal life already possessed in the darkness of faith, it brings the deepest and most complete fulfillment to the human person.

This means that the temporal unfolding of a Christian life is not a matter of growing old, of slowly deteriorating energy that slowly ends in death. The Christian's earthly life is the building up of a more beautiful future on the foundations of a present filled with the hidden power of eternity. It is drawn toward a life beyond death that is immune to decline or decay. Hope reverses the direction of temporal duration. Instead of being engulfed in the past, time flies toward a mysterious future where not an iota of its ephemeral flow will be lost, providing it is possessed by divine grace.

According to this notion of time, the Christian awakens each morning not with the weight of the preceding day added to all the others, but with a zest to discover new opportunities to live more fully today than yesterday. Each day offers him the chance to be reborn to hope, to enrich his life and develop its potential. Spiritual lassitude would paralyze him, whereas hope mobilizes all his vital forces.

We are not speaking here of a purely human psychological attitude.[2] This is not a matter of autosuggestion for the sake of stimulating enthusiasm for one's work, nor is it a temperamental disposition cultivated in order to confront life's difficulties more resolutely. Hope is first and above all rooted in God. It is from God that we await deliverance from the weight of the past, forgiveness for our sins, the grace to make a new start, and the assurance that we are advancing despite our weaknesses. It is God, the master of all duration, who has turned time around, so that it no longer moves inexorably toward death but toward immortality.

God never ceases bringing forth a new creation within

the old. Man's role is to accept this new creation, to allow God to make him over. Through hope he receives a new youth from above that makes him share fully in the transformation of mankind. Hope keeps alive his quest for happiness, and by deepening his faith in the beatitudes, gives him immediate access to happiness.

Hope is the measure of the vitality not only of the individual but of the entire Christian community. The more fervently the Church looks to the future, the more fully it lives. When it becomes too exclusively attached to the past, it can no longer use all its vital energies for the formation of a new humanity. Instead, it tends to focus its efforts on defending its structures or customs rather than broadcasting the seeds of its superior life throughout society.

Therefore, the living Church is one that hopes and leads man along the path of hope. Filled with confidence in the future promised by God, it actively collaborates in bringing this future to pass. It goes forward boldly, encouraging inquiry, new experiences, and creative efforts to understand and adapt the Gospel.

All in all, the Church is hope in concrete form already making the future of mankind real here and now. The Church exists and develops in the measure that hope takes on substance within it. It needs to constantly reroot itself in hope, so as to express it in all its actions, as well as in its structures and directives. It must also ask itself whether it really presents the authentic face of hope to the world, while not forgetting that each individual Christian shares in the responsibility to reflect this hope.

The Eyes of Hope

Much has been said about the eyes of faith, about the

supernatural sight that perceives divine realities and the mystery of salvation. Less has been said about the eyes of hope.

Hope gives us eyes to discern the direction of God's work within the world. It helps us to grasp the goal of this work and evaluate all things in the light of this goal.

Quite as piercing as the eyes of faith are the eyes of hope. They penetrate the mystery of man's future destiny. Just as the eyes of the man of faith discern the invisible in the visible, so the eyes of the man of hope glimpse the brilliant daylight of the future through the heavy mists of the present.

Every Christian should ask himself if he really has eyes of hope. Does his sight tend to be limited to immediate, verifiable realities? Can he glimpse, beyond the often disheartening situations in which he finds himself, an incomparably better world to come?

To perceive the goal is to try to perceive everything that precedes it and everything that leads to it. In the countless events and circumstances that make up the web of our present life, a superior plan comes into view. Things that have seemed disconcerting, the result of chance, take on a secret meaning to be fully known later on, but perceptible even now. The final end of the universe throws light on its present stage of development, and enables us more easily to find the thread that mysteriously links and coordinates all aspects of human life.

Hope thus makes possible an existential interpretation of all we see and experience. Through hope we see everything that exists in the light of what does not yet exist. We might say that hope grasps the unfolding of reality because it already contemplates the final state toward which reality is proceeding.

J. Moltmann has applied to hope Saint Anselm's famous definition of theology: "Faith in search of understanding."[3] Theology is faith that wants to see more clearly; it is the act of the believer seeking to penetrate the mystery of his faith through intellectual effort. When the object of theology becomes eschatology, a parallel formula is in order: "hope in search of understanding." Like faith, hope wants to understand its object. It stimulates the mind to encompass more fully the final realities.

That is why hope is a wellspring of doctrinal inquiry. But let us quickly add that such inquiry involves more than working out a doctrine of eschatology or the last things. When we speak of the eyes of hope, we are especially concerned with a way of looking at things, a mentality or point of view that influences our whole mode of thought.

Let us take a commonplace example. The Christian who reads his newspaper every day does not usually find much to sustain or increase his hope. Most of the news relates to political and social conflicts, to tragic events and acts of violence. This suggests a most disheartening view of mankind. Yet within this mass of disturbing facts, the eyes of hope manage to discover evidence of the strivings and advances of humanity as it is drawn upward. Many encouraging signs emerge from the shadows when we see with the eyes of hope. Conflicts are the price of progress. Disasters inspire generous efforts on behalf of their victims. The successes of violence are only apparent, and evil often becomes the occasion for a greater good, for redemption or forgiveness. The newspaper merely skims the surface of events. Hope enables us to grasp their underlying meaning, their contribution to the work of man's salvation.

Is not such an interpretation of facts somewhat arbitrary? There are those who would reject it, keeping their eyes stubbornly glued to the material content of the facts, to their literal description. Actually, the eyes of hope perceive the real import of events because they glimpse God's plan of salvation within them. If we believe in this divine plan, we will also admit there is more to these events than appears to an eyewitness or a newswriter. They are all caught up in a supernatural design.

From this point of view, we can see the value of the typological interpretation so often adopted by the Church Fathers in their commentaries on Scripture. It has led to many excesses, to inappropriate or improbable exegeses. Yet it has also had the essential merit of showing that the total meaning of Scripture is not limited to the literal sense of the text and that it can be established only in the light of God's entire plan for salvation. This plan is the supreme rule of hermeneutics, the guide to the interpretation of Scripture texts.

The Old Testament obviously needs to be read with the eyes of hope, to discover the reality ultimately envisioned as expressed in the promise. The value of the account of the Flood lies in the fact that it outlines the drama of salvation. Noah's true significance appears as a figure of Christ. The manna announced the Eucharist. According to the intention of the Holy Spirit, the two literary creations of Judith and Esther were inspired by the hope of an ideal woman who would play a decisive role in the salvation of the people of God. For the intent of the Spirit goes beyond the views of the writers themselves.

The New Testament must likewise be understood in the light of hope. The eschatological dimension is essential to the total message of Christ and must guide its interpretation. Here we have an eschatology in process of fulfillment that has already centered on the major event of the Redemption, but will continue to unfold until the last days. Jesus' words and actions, recorded in the Gospel, need to be accepted and meditated upon not only in faith but also in hope. For example, the parable of the Good Samaritan can be understood in all its power only when it is situated within the context of the Church's progress toward a future in which the supreme gift of love is more perfectly realized and toward a universal brotherhood in which all men eagerly succor the sufferings they encounter on the road of life.

What is true of Sacred Scripture is equally true of that other "scripture" of God and men that is history. The general history of the world's peoples must be read in the light of hope which alone can discern the secret of its development and its fundamental direction. The history of each individual person must likewise be viewed in the context of God's plan. It is completely polarized toward a future that throws light on its every phase, its apparent detours, its halts and leaps forward.

Looking at his past or his present, a Christian can decipher its meaning only by looking at it with the eyes of hope. Through hope he can better grasp the meaning of even the most obscure and incomprehensible events, including those that seem quite absurd. Certainly, the eyes of hope cannot understand everything or completely dispel the mystery, but they at least catch a glimpse of the end-term toward which all of history and all of life are moving, and discern a few beacons to light the way.

Hope and Optimism

Optimism is the translation of hope into one's mode of thinking.

But first of all, let us come to an agreement as to the meaning of the word "optimism." There are those who define optimism as an instinctive attitude tending to look only at the good side of things and to disregard their less favorable aspects. Such an attitude may well be called naïve, or at the very least partial and unilateral. It does not correspond to the total truth.

Such is not the optimism that springs from Christian

hope. This optimism does not hesitate to look evil straight in the face, whether among individuals or groups. It strives to be realistic, and not gloss over any part of reality. It does not focus solely on those aspects of the universe that are attuned to its aspirations. Far more, Christian optimism acknowledges the power of sin, a power all the more pervasive and disastrous in the measure that it cannot be discerned in visible facts. Optimism knows there are hidden evils, hypocrisies no one suspects, egoisms disguised under the most honorable external appearances.

Nonetheless, it remains optimism because it is founded on the victory of the risen Christ: "But take courage! I have overcome the world" (Jn 16:33). Powerful as sin may be, it is under the dominion of a still more powerful force. And so the final victor is not evil but the Savior: "despite the increase of sin, grace has far surpassed it" (Rm 5:20). Even while admitting the terrible proliferation of sin we must affirm even more forcefully the superabundance of salvation.

Pessimism, which is an expression of despair, sees only the spectacle of the evil, of all the deficiencies and failures of men. It is terrified by the extent of these evils, and tends to remember only the increasing domination of sin in the history of mankind. The present always seems decadent by comparison with previous epochs. Even in the Church there are manifestations of this pessimism with the propensity to think of the present as the most critical, the most calamitous of times from the religious point of view that the world has ever known.

Optimism, on the contrary, displays a far superior lucidity in the realm of faith, relying on irrefutable certitudes such as the following. The love of Christ will continue to win more victories over evil, until the perfect triumph of eternity. Under the inspiration of the Savior's grace, mankind is in process not of a descent but of a slow ascent toward the Father. The Church is continually extending its influence and deepening its holiness. All trials can lead to greater happiness.

Christian education should provide a sound formation in optimism, to encourage attitudes of supernatural hope in the face of life's disheartening realities. Such attitudes are most important in strengthening the Christian's commitment to the work of building a better world. To dedicate ourselves to improving the world's conditions, we must hope in the possibility of such improvement. To accept, through pessimism or despair, the view that the world is becoming worse or is doomed to succumb to evil, is to become the accomplice of those who make it evil, and to renounce in advance the fullest possible collaboration in the progress of mankind.

For that matter, even theology has not always followed the path of Christian optimism. We might point, for example, to the notion long held by the majority of theologians that the number of the elect is very limited. The opinion that only a minority, or even a very small minority, will attain salvation implies the victory of evil over the grace of salvation in the great majority of human lives. It concludes to a disastrous failure of God's plan and of the risen Christ.

No less pessimistic were the opinions expressed on the exclusion of non-Christians from salvation, and on the relegation to limbo of children who die without baptism. These theological positions of earlier centuries show us that the optimism of Christian thinking has to be achieved by slow degrees. The power of hope needs much time to penetrate theological thought. It will take the entire life cycle of the Church for hope to develop all its consequences in Christian doctrine. Christian hope will attain its "pleroma," its plenitude, only at the end of the world.

There is still much progress to be made in the think-

ing both of the Church and of individual Christians if
we are to arrive at an optimism which expresses the
whole truth of hope.

A Morality of Hope

In the area of moral doctrine, we need to return to
the point of view that hope must be considered as a wellspring of all the virtues.

We can then come to see the whole of human conduct,
as well as its individual problems, from the angle of
hope. Was this not Jesus' approach when he formulated
the ideals for human behavior in the Beatitudes? While
he certainly retained the essentials of the commandments
of the Old Law, he brought something new: the sense
of an imitation of the Father's perfect love (Mt 5:44-48).
As a stimulus to this leap beyond merely human stand-
ards and to all the sacrifices implicit in our involvement
in the mystery of the Redemption, he promised the happiness of the kingdom.

Christian morality is too often presented in the context of the Ten Commandments, as a series of regulations
to be observed under pain of the most severe penalties.
It is imbued with a spirit of fear, that Paul contrasts to
the filial adoption which makes us cry out "Abba!" (Rm
8:15).

The word "Abba" implies a hope that can give morality a totally different aspect, a more evangelical aspect
that conforms more closely to Christ.

First of all, the filial cry presupposes that we already
possess the Father's salvific love, and that the hope most
essential to man has begun to stir in our hearts. This love
has come to us in Christ and was rooted in our hearts
by the Spirit. Once this is granted, Christian behavior is
seen as the expansion of this love that strives to guide

all human actions. It remains obedience to the Father's will, but to a will that has taken possession of us through love.

Besides, the filial cry implies the eschatological situation which places us within the Resurrection and Ascension of Christ. As Paul says, God "raised us up and gave us a place in the heavens" (Ep 2:6). And so we are not mere pilgrims trudging toward the Father, and the moral problem does not consist strictly in knowing what we must do in order to be united to the Father in the world beyond. We already possess "a place in the heavens" within the darkness of our earthly life. The problem is to know how to develop to the maximum what is already in us so that our fellowship with the Father in eternal life can attain the full stature our present condition already contains germinally. Morality then becomes more akin to mysticism, the flourishing of the spiritual life planted in us by the Holy Spirit.[4]

Assured of this interior strength, morality can then give inventiveness greater leeway. The spirit of a morality founded on regulations tends to envelop all human actions and situations in the most absolute and detailed application of God's eternal law. The ideal commandment dictates behavior even to its smallest details. The morality of hope has no need of such predetermination, for it knows that the Christian possesses resources of grace sufficient to confront the future, and is armed with the inspirations of the Spirit in his search for the best way to follow. This inspiration does not come to him solely through his own thoughts. It is given to him as well through the Church's thinking. This means that the Christian cannot disregard the essential orientations and principles of the Church's code of morals. At the same time, the Spirit's inspiration, as in the case of the sacred books, is not dictated word by word, but stimulates to creativity in the search for solutions.

Finally, the morality of hope aspires to an ever more complete possession of the kingdom. The Beatitudes are not intended to promote a self-interested morality focussing on the pursuit of rewards. The happiness they promise in this life and in the life to come consists in the most disinterested love possible and in a renouncement of all human "possessions." But the climate of Christian life demands a strong desire for this unparalleled happiness and the certitude that it can indeed be attained. This is the opposite of fear of punishment, and nurtures profound serenity in accepting the demands of total self-giving.

Hope and Fear

Does Christian hope harbor an element of fear?

The answer to this question might seem to be in the affirmative.[5] Actually, the Christian's hope of eternal happiness cannot imply absolute certainty of achieving it. No man or woman is sure not to fall into serious sin. All of us must therefore maintain a fear of falling from grace and incurring God's judgment. To cast this fear aside would be dangerous presumption. The numerous passages on the "fear of the Lord" in the Old Testament confirm this way of thinking.

Nevertheless, the Gospel manifests progress on this point by comparison with the mentality of the Old Covenant. At the Annunciation, the message given to Mary was: "Do not fear!" (Lk 1:30). This was also Jesus' message to his disciples (Mk 6:50; Mt 14:27; Jn 6:20). After his Resurrection, Christ clearly sought to banish fear (cf. Mt 28:10) and to bring peace to his disciples troubled by his apparitions.

Paul grasped the advances in Christian mentality when he contrasted the spirit of fear with the spirit of filial adoption (cf. Rm 8:15). We find the most decisive expression of this approach in John's First Epistle: "Love has no room for fear; rather, perfect love casts out all fear. And since fear has to do with punishment, love is not yet perfect in one who is afraid" (1 Jn 4:18). Fear hobbles love, for it holds man back from God. It does not allow man to enter fully into fellowship with the Father.

Fear likewise prevents hope from attaining its full stature. To be authentic, hope must be founded on trust, and trust excludes fear. In the measure that we fear, our hope loses its power and assurance.

What, then, of the fear that would appear legitimate and necessary, the fear of the man who knows he is a sinner prone to fall, and who dreads God's judgment? Let us begin by saying that this fear concerns individuals only, since it relates to the possibility of falling from grace and losing the happiness of heaven. Now hope, as we have already stressed, is fundamentally communitarian. In the pursuit of its goals, the gathering of a community in heaven and the expansion of the Church upon earth, hope need have no fear of ultimate failure. The collective hope of mankind will be fulfilled beyond any shadow of a doubt.

Where individuals are concerned, we must clearly specify the kind of fear that exists. Strictly speaking, it is fear addressed to the individual man's weakness, and not a fear relating directly to God. The Christian dreads his own cowardice, lack of constancy or fidelity, and fear of sacrifice. Now, awareness of his frailty should normally lead him to put all his trust in the Lord. Far from making him dread God, it should induce him to abandon himself more completely to the Father's merciful goodness. To fear God would in a sense amount to seeing him as a dangerous adversary. While authentic hope acknowledges the possibility of straying and sinning, it turns toward the Father in a movement of love that strives to banish fear.

Training in the fear of God was an integral part of Old Testament teaching during a period of transition when hope was kept alive only by the promise. When the hour came for the promise to be fulfilled and the power to obey the law was given by the Spirit who dwells in the heart, fear ceased to be the goad to fidelity. Love inwardly possessed became the predominant attitude. The more this love grew the more hope banished fear. Now, what is true for the New Covenant in general is true as well in the personal life of each Christian. In the measure that the Christian allows himself to be seized by the Spirit of love, his hope overcomes all fear and is translated into total trust in the merciful goodness of God the Father.

Hope and The Apostolate

Hope played an important role in Paul's apostolic labors.

It inspired him to gather up the nations into the kingdom so that the glorious triumph of Christ might be consummated in the Parousia. Paul's was a hope with universal horizons, that already envisioned the acceptance of the Gospel message by all the peoples of the earth (cf. Rm 11:25).

To hold fast to such a perspective requires constantly renewed effort. Those who have been called to apostolic work might easily be tempted to restrict their hope to the specific apostolates entrusted to them. If on the contrary the hope of the Church lives in an apostle, he envisions the totality of the work to be done and sees his own task as a contribution to the far-flung development of the entire Christian community. The apostle is conscious of working for "the consummation of the world."

Hope thus inspires the apostle with an attitude of openness to everyone. Realizing that he is committed to a work meant to bring salvation to all, he can make no exclusions.

Like Paul, the apostle is invited to make himself all things to all men (cf. 1 Cor 9:22), so as to earn access to the Gospel message for everyone. This involves a motive of love, but also an attitude of hope. For the love addressed to all human beings is illumined by the hope of helping each one of them to accept salvation.

Hope nourishes in the apostle the conviction that his own individual task, modest as it may be, contributes to the real progress of history. Since the time span of human history is measured by the expansion of the Church throughout the world, every effort to extend the kingdom of Christ, even in a small way, hastens the final moment and brings history closer to its final end. Such a conviction is especially necessary because the apostle who has dedicated himself to a spiritual kingdom may have the impression he is laboring on the periphery of history, since his activities do not always produce visible and immediate results. However, the progress of mankind is above all a progress of the spirit, and this is where the apostle's work is truly efficacious.

While apostolic hope has a universal perspective, it is directed in a special way to the apostle's particular field of labor. Hope is a primordial condition for his energetic activity, "for the plowman should plow in hope" (1 Cor 9:10). In Paul's Letters we often come across references to his hopes for the Christian communities among which he worked. To the Thessalonians, he wrote: "Who, after all, if not you, will be our hope or joy?" (I Th 2:19). We know there were times when Paul was grieved to see his apostolic hopes disappointed. The most poignant of these was doubtless the occasion when he preached in the Areopagus of Athens (cf. Ac 17:32-35). This failure caused him great sadness (cf. 1 Cor 2:3). What happened to Paul is bound to happen in the course of every apostolic mission. But the apostle possesses a hope capable of surviving any number of disappointments and making a new start when his efforts have not reaped the expected harvest.

Moreover, Paul vigorously affirmed his confidence in his mission to carry out the "ministry of the Spirit," which was far superior to the ministry of Moses in the Old Testament. He declared he was filled with such buoyant hope that he had no reason to grow faint or turn back in shame. Christ, through the Spirit, made Paul's actions productive (cf. 2 Cor 3:1-18). The efficacious presence of the Holy Spirit is a source of steadfastness and boldness for every apostle.

Equally indicative of the grandeur of the apostolate is the hope for which Paul proclaimed he had been condemned and imprisoned. "I find myself on trial now because of my hope in the resurrection of the dead" (Ac 23:6; cf. 26:6-7). The final goal of apostolic hope is the universal resurrection, proof that hope expects everything from God. But while it waits, hope does not remain passive. It inspires the apostle to act and to accept suffering in order to obtain the life of resurrection for all mankind.

The final resurrection is not desired for its own sake alone. It will inaugurate Christ's definitive and total ascendancy over humanity. The object of Christian hope is this kingdom of Christ. That is why the supreme cry of hope is a cry of love: "Come, Lord Jesus!" (Rv 22:20). This "Come!" resounds with such vehemence because it calls not only for the Parousia but also for the coming of the Lord into our world through the witness of the Church, a witness that has already begun. Those who already possess the hidden reality of this coming and enjoy its fruits live in the hope of seeing it even more resplendent and complete.

NOTES FOR CHAPTER EIGHT

1. Cf. Van der Ploeg, "L'espérance dans l'Ancien Testament," **Revue Biblique**, 1954, pp. 483-4.
2. G. Marcel insisted on this point in **Structure de l'espérance, Dieu vivant**, pp. 19, 79.
3. **Théologie de l'espérance**, pp. 31-34.
4. "Ethics becomes, in its essentials, fidelity to an already heavenly condition. . . . Our inclusion in Jesus Christ is so deeply rooted in the eternal, our resurrection in him is so real, our presence at his side in heaven is so close and certain that Paul, without abolishing hope or the humble fear of failing, can reverse the polarity of the Christian life. The question now is less how to make ascetic efforts converge toward a goal than to make the spiritual plenitude of a grace already conferred radiate far and wide. The incentive to progress is less one of indigence than of riches, less the need for a superabundance than the dynamism of an over-flowing spiritual life," (G. Didier, **Désintéressement du chrétien, La rétribution morale du chrétien**, Paris, 1955, p. 191).
5. Various positions have been adopted by Tradition. St. Augustine juxtaposed hope and fear as contradictory attitudes, whereas St. Gregory the Great saw them as co-existing at two different levels of the soul (Delhaye-Boulangé, **Espérance et vie chrétienne**, p. 149). St. Thomas associates hope with filial fear, which is different from servile fear (cf. C. A. Bernard, **Théologie de l'espérance**, pp. 133-141).